THE FIRST ENGLISH
PRAYER BOOK

THE FIRST
ENGLISH
PRAYER BOOK

1999

ARTHUR JAMES
NEW ALRESFORD

MOREHOUSE PUBLISHING
HARRISBURG, PA

First published in Great Britain by
ARTHUR JAMES
an imprint of
JOHN HUNT PUBLISHING
46a West Street,
New Alresford, Hants SO24 9AU
United Kingdom

First published in USA and Canada by Morehouse Publishing
PO Box 1321, Harrisburg, Pennsylvania 17105 USA
Morehouse Publishing is a division of the Morehouse Group

A catalogue record for this book is available
from the British Library

ISBN 0 85305 479 7

Typeset in Monotype Joanna
by Strathmore Publishing Services, London N7

Printed and bound in Singapore

CONTENTS

INTRODUCTION

The attractions of The First English Prayer Book are as great today as at any time since its publication in 1549. There is growing interest in the English spiritual tradition; The First English Prayer Book was fed by the best of medieval English spirituality, and after the Reformation became the main source of spiritual nourishment for the common people of England. There is also a growing need and desire, especially in the thousands of ancient churches scattered across the English countryside, for forms of worship which lay people can lead; The First English Prayer Book is ideally suited to this purpose, and in past centuries has sustained many parishes without a resident priest. And as the different denominations move closer together, The First English Prayer Book should be valued as a means of enhancing the ecumenical spirit.

Past
The main compiler of The First English Prayer Book was Thomas Cranmer, who was appointed Archbishop of Canterbury by King Henry VIII, and continued to serve through the reign of his young successor, King Edward VI. Cranmer was from the outset committed to making worship comprehensible, by introducing services in the mother tongue. King Henry, however, continued to prefer the old Latin services; and so, despite breaking with the Pope, he hampered the process of

reform. In 1542 Cranmer persuaded the King to allow a passage from the New Testament to be read in English in parish churches on Sunday; and a year later Cranmer produced an English version of the Litany, a long series of prayers and responses to be said or sung in processions. Otherwise he had to work in secret, preparing English services for the eyes of a more sympathetic monarch in the future.

When Edward became king in 1547, a committee was immediately formed under Cranmer's leadership to produce an entire service book in English. In December the following year it was submitted to Parliament for approval; and three months later, in the spring of 1549, printed copies went on sale – two shillings for the paperback edition, and three shillings and fourpence for the edition in hard covers. While the main text of the services was printed in black, the instructions were in red, and hence became known as 'rubrics'.

The English language had entered the most vivid and majestic phase of its evolution, and Cranmer was the master of it. So the people of England soon learned to love the poetic phrases and cadences of their new service book. They were also reassured that no new ideas or rituals were being foisted on them. On the contrary, Cranmer followed closely the medieval forms of worship, especially the Old Sarum rites. His vision was most clearly expressed in the services of Matins and Evensong, which were truncated forms of the old monastic daily office: Cranmer wanted corporate prayer no longer to be the preserve of monks, nuns and priests, but to be shared by everyone.

In his combination of populism and conservatism Cranmer was typically English. But he was soon overwhelmed by cries for more extreme reform from clergy committed to the Protestant cause. Thus in 1552 *The Second English Prayer Book* was published, with less ritual, and with verbal alterations to fit Protestant theology. These changes included the addition of a confession and curiously half-hearted absolution at the start of Matins and Evensong. There was also pressure to eliminate the giving of a ring at marriage; but after heated debate this was retained.

The brief reign of Queen Mary saw the return of the Latin Mass, and the burning at the stake of Cranmer, along with several other church leaders. After Queen Elizabeth's accession in 1558 the two forms of *The Prayer Book* were favoured by rival groups: the more strongly Protestant clergy preferred the 1552 revision, while those who valued continuity with the medieval past upheld the first version. In the Civil War *The Prayer Book* was a focus of hostility, with many Parliamentarians wishing to abandon all forms of liturgy; and after their victory they declared *The Prayer Book* illegal, replacing it with a *Directory* which merely gave broad instructions as to how worship should be conducted.

When the monarchy was restored in 1660, King Charles II, along with many bishops and clergy, declared his devotion to Cranmer's *First English Prayer Book*. But in a spirit of reconciliation he ordered that a conference be convened, to revise the services in such a way as to be acceptable to all sides. The result, published in 1662, was far closer to the 1552 version. Nonetheless clergy with strong Protestant views remained dissatisfied, and some broke away to form new denominations.

Two centuries later the Tractarian movement reawakened the Church of England to its medieval heritage. And in many churches rituals and prayers from *The First English Prayer Book*, which had been cut out, began to be included again. And this process was given episcopal blessing in the revision proposed in 1928, in which most of these rituals and prayers were offered as 'alternatives'. This revision failed to gain parliamentary approval, but it soon became widely followed – even to the extent of the Archbishop of Canterbury using the 1928 form at the wedding of Prince Charles and Lady Diana Spencer.

Present

Through its origins in medieval liturgy *The First English Prayer Book* may be regarded as truly Catholic. And since it ushered in the Reformation, enabling the laity to participate in public worship, it is the common root of every denomination in England. Thus its use is appropriate in worship attended by people of different denominations. This includes not only special ecumenical gatherings, but also the regular services of numerous rural communities where the parish church is the only place of worship.

More importantly, *The First English Prayer Book* is a means – perhaps the only means – of preserving worship in England's country churches. In the early years of Queen Victoria's reign virtually every parish was able, for the first time in many centuries, to have its own resident priest. But within a few decades this luxury was being undermined by falling church incomes with which to pay the clergy, and later by falling numbers of people offering themselves as clergy. So now most smaller rural communities again find themselves without a local parson, and being served by a priest living elsewhere who is struggling to cover several parishes. As a result in many places there are dwindling numbers of worshippers, and fewer services for them to attend.

The First English Prayer Book meets this situation perfectly, by enabling lay people to conduct many of the services. In specifying who should lead the services Cranmer made a clear distinction between a 'priest', who should be ordained, and a 'minister', who may be ordained or lay. The only service which requires a priest – and a bishop – is that of Confirmation; all other services can be conducted by a lay person. Even the Holy Communion may be led by a lay person if the reserved sacrament, previously consecrated by a priest, is administered. Moreover, The First English Prayer Book satisfies rural spiritual tastes, which tend to be conservative.

There is perhaps another advantage of The First English Prayer Book – of which Cranmer would probably not approve. Today many people find orthodox Christian belief difficult, but continue to desire the spiritual sustenance which worship can provide. Cranmer expresses eternal truth in language as sublime as that of Shakespeare, which can be appreciated, without being taken literally, by the devout sceptic. Thus it may draw into church many who would not count themselves as believers.

A common complaint of the 1662 version is that it is hard to follow, and hence also difficult to conduct. The printing of the rubrics in red in *The First English Prayer Book* was designed to encourage all literate people to become familiar with the text, and to enable laity with little or no training to lead worship. It is hoped that the present edition, with some revisions to the rubrics and the exclusion of some more obscure prayers, is even easier to use.

MATINS

The minister shall begin with a loud voice:

Minister	O Lord, open thou my lips;
All	**And my mouth shall show forth thy praise.**
Minister	O God, make speed to save me;
All	**O Lord, make haste to help me.**
Minister	Glory be to the Father, and to the Son, and to the Holy Ghost;
All	**As it was in the beginning, is now, and ever shall be, world without end. Amen.**
Minister	Praise ye the Lord;
All	**Alleluia.**

Then may be said or sung a psalm or hymn.

The minister, or the person that is appointed, shall read the first lesson.

Then shall be said or sung the Te Deum Laudamus.

TE DEUM LAUDAMUS

We praise thee, O God : we acknowledge thee to be the Lord.

All the earth doth worship thee : the Father everlasting.

To thee all angels cry aloud : the heavens and all the powers therein.

To thee Cherubin, and Seraphin : continually do cry.

Holy, holy, holy : Lord God of Sabaoth;

Heaven and earth are full of the majesty : of thy glory.

The glorious company of the apostles : praise thee.

The goodly fellowship of the prophets : praise thee.

The noble army of martyrs : praise thee.

The holy church throughout all the world :
doth acknowledge thee;

The Father : of an infinite majesty;

Thine honourable, true : and only Son;

Also the Holy Ghost : the comforter.

Thou art the king of glory : O Christ.

Thou art the everlasting Son : of the Father.

When thou tookest upon thee to deliver man :
thou didst not abhor the Virgin's womb.

When thou hadst overcome the sharpness of death :
thou didst open the kingdom of heaven to all believers.

Thou sittest at the right hand of God : in the glory of
the Father.

We believe that thou shalt come : to be our judge.

We therefore pray thee, help thy servants : whom thou
hast redeemed with thy precious blood.

Make them to be numbered with thy saints : in glory
everlasting.

O Lord, save thy people : and bless thine heritage.

Govern them : and lift them up for ever.

Day by day : we magnify thee;

And we worship thy name : ever world without end.

Vouchsafe, O Lord : to keep us this day without sin.

O Lord, have mercy upon us : have mercy upon us.

O Lord, let thy mercy lighten upon us : as our trust is in thee.

O Lord, in thee have I trusted : let me never be confounded.

Then the minister, or the person that is appointed, shall read the second lesson.

Then shall be said or sung the Benedictus.

BENEDICTUS

Blessed be the Lord God of Israel : for he hath visited and redeemed his people;

And hath raised up a mighty salvation for us : in the house of his servant David;

As he spake by the mouth of his holy prophets : which have been since the world began;

That we should be saved from our enemies : and from the hands of all that hate us;

To perform the mercy promised to our forefathers : and to remember his holy covenant;

To perform the oath which he sware to our forefather Abraham : that he would give us;

That we being delivered out of the hands of our enemies : might serve him without fear;

In holiness and righteousness before him : all the days of our life.

And thou, child, shalt be called the Prophet of the
Highest : for thou shalt go before the face of the Lord to
prepare his ways;

To give knowledge of salvation unto his people :
for the remission of their sins;

Through the tender mercy of our God : whereby the
day-spring from on high hath visited us;

To give light to them that sit in darkness, and in the
shadow of death : and to guide our feet into the way of
peace.

Glory be to the Father, and to the Son : and to the
Holy Ghost;

As it was in the beginning, is now, and ever shall be :
world without end. Amen.

Then shall be said the Creed.

Minister   I believe in God
**All   the Father Almighty, maker of heaven and
             earth. And in Jesus Christ his only Son our
             Lord, who was conceived by the Holy
             Ghost, born of the Virgin Mary, suffered
             under Pontius Pilate, was crucified, dead,
             and buried. He descended into hell. The
             third day he rose again from the dead.
             He ascended into heaven, and sitteth on
             the right hand of God the Father almighty.
             From thence he shall come to judge the
             quick and the dead. I believe in the Holy
             Ghost; the holy catholic church;**

the communion of saints; the forgiveness of sins; the resurrection of the body, and the life everlasting. Amen.

Then shall be said the prayers following:

Minister	Let us pray.
	Lord, have mercy upon us.
All	**Christ, have mercy upon us.**
Minister	Lord, have mercy upon us.
All	**Our Father, which art in heaven, hallowed be thy name. Thy kingdom come. Thy will be done in earth as it is in heaven. Give us this day our daily bread. And forgive us our trespasses, as we forgive them that trespass against us. And lead us not into temptation, but deliver us from evil. Amen.**
Minister	O Lord, show thy mercy upon us;
All	**And grant us thy salvation.**
Minister	O Lord, save the king/queen;
All	**And mercifully hear us when we call upon thee.**
Minister	Endue thy ministers with righteousness;
All	**And make thy chosen people joyful.**
Minister	O Lord, save thy people;
All	**And bless thine inheritance.**
Minister	Give peace in our time, O Lord;
All	**Because there is none other that fighteth for us, but only thou, O God.**

Minister	O God, make clean our hearts within us;
All	**And take not thy Holy Spirit from us.**
Minister	The Lord be with you;
All	**And with thy spirit.**

Then shall follow three collects: the first of the day, the second for peace, the third for grace to live well.

THE COLLECT OF THE DAY

THE SECOND COLLECT: FOR PEACE

Minister O God, who art author of peace, and lover of concord, in knowledge of whom standeth our eternal life, whose service is perfect freedom: defend us, thy humble servants, in all assaults of our enemies, that we surely trusting in thy defence, may not fear the power of any adversaries; through the might of Jesus Christ our Lord. **Amen.**

THE THIRD COLLECT: FOR GRACE

Minister O Lord, our heavenly Father, almighty and everliving God, which hast safely brought us to the beginning of this day: defend us in the same with thy mighty power; and grant that this day we fall into no sin, neither run into any kind of danger, but that all our doings may be ordered by thy governance, to do always that is righteous in thy sight; through Jesus Christ our Lord. **Amen.**

A sermon or homily may follow. Then the minister or a person that is appointed, may say prayers.

EVENSONG

The minister shall begin with a loud voice:

Minister   O Lord, open thou my lips;
All   **And my mouth shall show forth thy praise.**
Minister   O God, make speed to save me;
All   **O Lord, make haste to help me.**
Minister   Glory be to the Father, and to the Son, and to
           the Holy Ghost.
All   **As it was in the beginning, is now, and ever
           shall be, world without end. Amen.**
Minister   Praise ye the Lord;
All   **Alleluia.**

Then may be said or sung a psalm or hymn.

The minister, or the person that is appointed, shall
read the first lesson.

Then shall be said or sung the Magnificat:

MAGNIFICAT

My soul doth magnify the Lord : and my spirit hath
rejoiced in God my saviour.

   For he hath regarded : the lowliness of his hand-
maiden.

   For behold, from henceforth : all generations shall call
me blessed.

   For he that is mighty hath magnified me :
and holy is his name.

And his mercy is on them that fear him : throughout all generations.

He hath showed strength with his arm : he hath scattered the proud in the imagination of their hearts.

He hath put down the mighty from their seat : and hath exalted the humble and meek.

He hath filled the hungry with good things : and the rich he hath sent empty away.

He remembering his mercy hath holpen his servant Israel : as he promised to our forefathers, Abraham and his seed for ever.

Glory be to the Father, and to the Son : and to the Holy Ghost;

As it was in the beginning, is now, and ever shall be : world without end. Amen.

The minister, or the person that is appointed, shall read the second lesson.

Then shall be said or sung the Nunc Dimittis.

NUNC DIMITTIS

Lord, now lettest thou thy servant depart in peace : according to thy word.

For mine eyes have seen : thy salvation,

Which thou hast prepared : before the face of all people;

To be a light to lighten the Gentiles : and to be the glory of thy people Israel.

Glory be to the Father, and to the Son : and to the Holy Ghost;

As it was in the beginning, is now, and ever shall be : world without end. Amen.

Then shall be said the Creed.

Minister   I believe in God

All   **the Father Almighty, maker of heaven and earth. And in Jesus Christ his only Son our Lord, who was conceived by the Holy Ghost, born of the Virgin Mary, suffered under Pontius Pilate, was crucified, dead, and buried. He descended into hell; the third day he rose again from the dead. He ascended into heaven, and sitteth on the right hand of God the Father almighty. From thence he shall come to judge the quick and the dead. I believe in the Holy Ghost; the holy catholic church; the communion of saints; the forgiveness of sins; the resurrection of the body, and the life everlasting. Amen.**

Then shall be said the prayers following:

Minister   Let us pray.
               Lord, have mercy upon us.

All   **Christ, have mercy upon us.**

Minister   Lord, have mercy upon us.

All	**Our Father, which art in heaven, hallowed be thy name. Thy kingdom come. Thy will be done in earth as it is in heaven. Give us this day our daily bread. And forgive us our trespasses, as we forgive them that trespass against us. And lead us not into temptation, but deliver us from evil. Amen.**
Minister	O Lord, show thy mercy upon us;
All	**And grant us thy salvation.**
Minister	O Lord, save the king/queen;
All	**And mercifully hear us when we call upon thee.**
Minister	Endue thy ministers with righteousness;
All	**And make thy chosen people joyful.**
Minister	O Lord, save thy people;
All	**And bless thine inheritance.**
Minister	Give peace in our time, O Lord;
All	**Because there is none other that fighteth for us, but only thou, O God.**
Minister	O God, make clean our hearts within us;
All	**And take not thy Holy Spirit from us.**
Minister	The Lord be with you;
All	**And with thy spirit.**

Then shall follow three collects. The first of the day, the second for peace, the third for aid against all perils.

THE COLLECT OF THE DAY

THE SECOND COLLECT: FOR PEACE

Minister   O God, from whom all holy desires, all good
           counsels, and all just works do proceed: give
           unto thy servants that peace which the world
           cannot give; that both our hearts may be set
           to obey thy commandments, and also that by
           thee we being defended from the fear of our
           enemies may pass our time in rest and quiet-
           ness; through the merits of Jesus Christ our
           saviour. **Amen.**

THE THIRD COLLECT:
FOR AID AGAINST ALL PERILS

Minister   Lighten our darkness, we beseech thee, O
           Lord; and by thy great mercy defend us from
           all perils and dangers of this night; for the
           love of thy only Son, our saviour, Jesus Christ.
           Amen.

A sermon or homily may follow. Then the minister or
a person that is appointed, may say prayers.

HOLY COMMUNION

The minister, turning toward the altar, shall say:

Minister   Almighty God,

All   **unto whom all hearts be open, and all desires known, and from whom no secrets are hid: cleanse the thoughts of our hearts by the inspiration of thy Holy Spirit; that we may perfectly love thee, and worthily magnify thy holy name; through Christ our Lord. Amen.**

The minister shall say:

Minister   Lord, have mercy upon us.

All   **Christ, have mercy upon us.**

Minister   Lord, have mercy upon us.

Then the minister shall begin:

Minister   Glory be to God on high,

All   **and in earth, peace, good will towards men. We praise thee, we bless thee, we worship thee, we glorify thee, we give thanks to thee for thy great glory, O Lord God, heavenly King, God the Father almighty. O Lord, the only begotten Son Jesu Christ: O Lord God, lamb of God, Son of the Father, that takest away the sins of the world, have mercy upon us. Thou that takest away the sins of the world, receive our prayer. Thou that sittest at the right hand of God the Father, have mercy upon us.**

For thou only art holy, thou only art the Lord; thou only, O Christ, with the Holy Ghost, art most high in the glory of God the Father. Amen.

Then the minister shall turn to the people and say:

Minister	The Lord be with you;
All	**And with thy spirit.**
Minister	Let us pray.

Then shall follow the collect of the day, with one of these two collects following, for the monarch:

Minister   Almighty God, whose kingdom is everlasting, and power infinite; have mercy upon the whole congregation, and so rule the heart of thy chosen servant [Name], our king/queen and governor, that s/he, knowing whose minister s/he is, may above all things seek thy honour and glory; and that we his/her subjects, duly considering whose authority s/he has, may faithfully serve, honour, and humbly obey him/her, in thee and for thee, according to thy blessed word and ordinance; through Jesus Christ our Lord, who with thee and the Holy Ghost, liveth and reigneth, ever one God, world without end. **Amen.**

Almighty and everlasting God, we be taught
by thy holy word, that the hearts of kings are
in thy rule and governance, and that thou dost
dispose and turn them as it seemeth best to
thy godly wisdom. We humbly beseech thee
so to dispose and govern the heart of [Name],
thy servant, our king/queen and governor,
that in all his/her thoughts, words and works,
s/he may ever seek thy honour and glory, and
study to preserve thy people, committed to
his/her charge, in wealth, peace and godliness.
Grant this, O merciful Father, for thy dear
Son's sake, Jesus Christ our Lord. **Amen.**

The minister, or the person that is appointed, shall
read the Epistle, saying:

The first/second/third Epistle of Saint [Name]
to [recipient], written in the [number] chapter.

The minister or the person that is appointed shall read
the Gospel, saying:

The holy Gospel, written in the [number]
chapter of the Gospel according to Saint
[Name]:

All   **Glory be to thee, O Lord.**

After the Gospel has ended the minister shall begin the
Creed:

Minister	I believe in one God,
All	**the Father almighty, maker of heaven and earth, and of all things visible and invisible. And in one Lord Jesus Christ, the only begotten Son of God, begotten of his Father before all worlds, God of God, light of light, very God of very God, begotten, not made, being of one substance with the Father, by whom all things were made: who for us men, and for our salvation came down from heaven, and was incarnate by the Holy Ghost of the Virgin Mary, and was made man, and was crucified also for us under Pontius Pilate. He suffered and was buried, and the third day he rose again according to the Scriptures, and ascended into heaven, and sitteth on the right hand of the Father. And he shall come again with glory to judge both the quick and the dead; whose kingdom shall have no end. And I believe in the Holy Ghost, the Lord and giver of life, who proceedeth from the Father and the Son, who with the Father and the Son together is worshipped and glorified, who spake by the prophets. And I believe one catholic and apostolic church. I acknowledge one baptism for the remission of sins. And I look for the resurrection of the dead, and the life of the world to come. Amen.**

Then shall follow the sermon or homily.

Then shall follow the Offertory. This sentence of holy Scripture may be said by the minister, before the people offer:

> Let your light so shine before men, that they may see your good works, and glorify your Father which is in heaven.

Then shall the minister take so much bread and wine, as shall suffice for the people.

Minister	The Lord be with you;
All	**And with thy spirit.**
Minister	Lift up your hearts;
All	**We lift them up unto the Lord.**
Minister	Let us give thanks to our Lord God;
All	**It is meet and right so to do.**
Minister	It is very meet, right and our bounden duty that we should at all times, and in all places give thanks to thee, O Lord, holy Father, almighty everlasting God.

Here shall follow the proper preface according to the time, if there be any specifically appointed. Then shall follow:

Minister	Therefore with angels and archangels, and with all the holy company of heaven, we laud and magnify thy glorious name, evermore praising thee, and saying:

All   Holy, holy, holy, Lord God of hosts: heaven and earth are full of thy glory; hosanna in the highest. Blessed is he that cometh in the name of the Lord. Glory to thee, O Lord in the highest.

Then turning to the people, the minister shall say:

Let us pray for the whole state of Christ's church.

Then the minister, or the person that is appointed, shall offer prayers. If the reserved sacrament is to be used, the minister shall go straight to the introduction to the Lord's Prayer.

Then the priest, turning him to the altar, shall say plainly:

O God, heavenly Father, which of thy tender mercy didst give thine only Son Jesus Christ to suffer death upon the cross for our redemption, who made there (by his one oblation once offered) a full, perfect and sufficient sacrifice, oblation, and satisfaction, for the sins of the whole world; and did institute, and in his holy gospel command us to celebrate, a perpetual memory of that his precious death, until his coming again. Hear us, O merciful Father, we beseech thee; and with thy Holy Spirit and word, vouchsafe to

Here the priest blesses the bread and wine.

bless and sanctify these thy gifts, and creatures of bread and wine, that they may be unto us the body and blood of thy most dearly beloved Son Jesus Christ.

Here the priest must take the bread into his hands.

Who in the same night that he was betrayed, took bread; and when he had blessed and given thanks, he brake it, and gave it to his disciples, saying: Take, eat, this is my body which is given for you; do this in remembrance of me.

Here the priest shall take the cup into his hands.

Likewise after supper he took the cup, and when he had given thanks, he gave it to them saying: Drink ye all of this, for this is my blood of the new testament, which is shed for you and for many, for the remission of sins; do this as oft as you shall drink it, in remembrance of me.

Then, showing the sacrament to the people, the priest shall say:

Wherefore, O Lord and heavenly Father, according to the instruction of thy dearly beloved Son, our saviour Jesus Christ, we thy humble servants do celebrate, and make here before thy divine majesty, with these thy holy gifts, the memory which thy Son hath willed us to make, having in remembrance his blessed passion, mighty resurrection, and glorious ascension, rendering unto thee most hearty thanks for the innumerable benefits procured unto us by the same, entirely desiring thy Fatherly goodness, mercifully to accept this our sacrifice of praise and thanksgiving; most humbly beseeching thee to grant that, by the merits and death of thy Son Jesus Christ, and through faith in his blood, we and all thy whole church may obtain remission of our sins, and all other benefits of his passion. And here we offer and present unto thee, O Lord, ourselves, our souls and bodies, to be a reasonable, holy and lively sacrifice unto thee; humbly beseeching thee, that whosoever shall be partakers of this holy communion, may worthily receive the most precious body and blood of thy Son Jesus Christ; and be fulfilled with thy grace and heavenly benediction, and made one body with thy Son Jesus Christ, that he may dwell in them, and they in him. And although we be unworthy, through our manifold sins, to offer unto thee any sacrifice; yet we beseech thee to accept this our bounden duty and service, and command these our prayers and supplications, by the ministry of thy holy angels, to be brought up into thy holy tabernacle before the sight of thy divine majesty, not weighing our merits, but pardoning our offences; through Christ our Lord, by whom, and with whom, in the unity of the Holy Ghost, all honour and glory, be unto thee, O Father almighty, world without end. **Amen.**

Minister　As our saviour Christ hath commanded and taught us, we are bold to say:

All　　**Our Father, which art in heaven, hallowed be thy name. Thy kingdom come. Thy will be done in earth as it is in heaven. Give us this day our daily bread. And forgive us our trespasses, as we forgive them that trespass against us. And lead us not into temptation, but deliver us from evil. Amen.**

Then shall the minister say:

Minister　The peace of the Lord be always with you.

All　　**And with thy spirit.**

Minister　Christ our Pascal lamb was offered up for us, once for all, when he bore our sins on his body upon the cross, for he is the very lamb of God, that taketh away the sins of the world; wherefore let us keep a joyful and holy feast with the Lord.

Here the minister shall turn him toward those that come to the Holy Communion, and shall say:

Ye that do truly and earnestly repent you of your sins to almighty God, and be in love and charity with your neighbours, and intend to

lead a new life, following the commandments
of God, and walking from henceforth in his
holy ways: draw near and take this holy
sacrament to your comfort; and make your
humble confession to almighty God, and to
his holy church here gathered together in his
name, meekly kneeling upon your knees.

Then shall the general confession be made, all humbly
kneeling upon their knees.

All   **Almighty God, Father of our Lord Jesus
Christ, maker of all things, judge of all
men, we acknowledge and bewail our
manifold sins and wickedness, which we
from time to time most grievously have
committed, by thought, word and deed,
against thy divine majesty, provoking most
justly thy wrath and indignation against us;
we do earnestly repent and are heartily
sorry for these our misdoings; the remembrance of them is grievous unto us, the
burden of them is intolerable. Have mercy
upon us, have mercy upon us, most merciful Father, for thy Son our Lord Jesus
Christ's sake; forgive us all that is past, and
grant that we may ever hereafter serve and
please thee in newness of life, to the
honour and glory of thy name; through
Jesus Christ our Lord.**

If there is no priest present, the following absolution shall not be said. If there is a priest present he shall stand up, and turning himself to the people, say thus:

Almighty God, our heavenly Father, who of his great mercy hath promised forgiveness of sins to all them, which with hearty repentance and true faith, turn unto him: have mercy upon you, pardon and deliver you from all your sins, confirm and strengthen you in all goodness, and bring you to everlasting life: through Jesus Christ our Lord. **Amen.**

Then shall the minister say:

Hear what comfortable words our saviour Christ saith, to all that truly turn to him:

Come unto me all that travail, and are heavy laden, and I shall refresh you. So God loved the world, that he gave his only begotten Son, to the end that all that believe in him, should not perish, but have life everlasting.

Hear also what Saint Paul saith:

This is a true saying, and worthy of all men to be received, that Jesus Christ came into this world to save sinners.

Hear also what Saint John saith:

If any man sin, we have an advocate with the Father, Jesus Christ the righteous, and he is the propitiation for our sins.

Then shall the minister turn himself to the altar and kneel down.

Minister   We do not presume

All   to come to this thy table, O merciful Lord, trusting in our own righteousness, but in thy manifold and great mercies. We are not worthy so much as to gather up the crumbs under thy table. But thou art the same Lord whose property is always to have mercy: grant us therefore, gracious Lord, so to eat the flesh of thy dear Son Jesus Christ, and to drink his blood in these holy mysteries, that we may continually dwell in him, and he in us, that our sinful bodies may be made clean by his body, and our souls washed through his most precious blood. Amen.

Then shall the minister say:

Minister   O lamb of God,

All   that takest away the sins of the world, have mercy upon us.

O lamb of God, that takest away the sins of the world, grant us thy peace.

Then shall the minister first receive the Communion in both kinds, and next deliver it to other ministers, if any be there present, and after to the people.

And when the minister delivereth the sacrament of the body of Christ, every one of these words shall be said:

> The body of our Lord Jesus Christ which was given for thee, preserve thy body and soul unto everlasting life.

And the minister delivering the sacrament of the blood shall say:

> The blood of our Lord Jesus Christ which was shed for thee, preserve thy body and soul unto everlasting life.

Then shall thanks to God be given.

Minister   The Lord be with you;

All   And with thy spirit.

Minister   Let us pray.

All   Almighty and everliving God, we most heartily thank thee, for that thou hast vouchsafed to feed us in these holy mysteries, with the spiritual food of the most precious body and blood of thy Son, our saviour Jesus Christ; and hast assured us, duly receiving the same, of thy favour and goodness towards us, and that we are very members incorporate in thy mystical body,

which is the blessed company of all faithful people, and heirs through hope of thy everlasting kingdom, by the merits of the most precious death and passion of thy dear Son. We therefore most humbly beseech thee, O heavenly Father, so to assist us with thy grace, that we may continue in that holy fellowship, and do all such good works as thou hast prepared for us to walk in; through Jesus Christ our Lord, to whom with thee and the Holy Ghost, be all honour and glory, world without end.

If there is no priest present, the following blessing shall not be said. If there is a priest present he, turning him to the people, shall let them depart with this blessing:

The peace of God, which passeth all understanding, keep your hearts and minds in the knowledge and love of God, and of his Son Jesus Christ our Lord; and the blessing of God almighty, the Father, the Son, and the Holy Ghost, be amongst you and remain with you always. **Amen.**

When the Holy Communion is celebrated on a workday, or in private houses, then may be omitted the Gloria, the Creed and the Homily.

The Sacrament may be reserved in a suitable receptacle for future services.

Here follows the proper prefaces according to the time, if there be any specially appointed:

PROPER PREFACES

Upon Christmas Day
Because thou didst give Jesus Christ, thine only Son, to be born at this day for us, who by the operation of the Holy Ghost, was made very man, of the substance of the Virgin Mary his mother, and that without spot of sin to make us clean from all sin. Therefore with angels, etc.

Upon Easter Day
But chiefly are we bound to praise thee, for the glorious resurrection of thy Son Jesus Christ, our Lord, for he is the very Pascal lamb, which was offered for us, and hath taken away the sin of the world; who by his death hath destroyed death, and by his rising to life again, hath restored to us everlasting life. Therefore with angels, etc.

Upon *Ascension Day*

Through thy most dear beloved Son, Jesus Christ our Lord, who after his most glorious resurrection manifestly appeared to all his disciples, and in their sight ascended up into heaven, to prepare a place for us, that where he is thither might we also ascend, and reign with him in glory. Therefore with angels, etc.

Upon *Whitsunday*

Through Jesus Christ our Lord, according to whose most true promise, the Holy Ghost came down this day from heaven with a sudden great sound, as it had been a mighty wind, in the likeness of fiery tongues, lighting upon the apostles, to teach them, and to lead them to all truth, giving them both the gift of diverse languages, and also boldness with fervent zeal, constantly to preach the Gospel unto all nations, whereby we are brought out of darkness and error, into the clear light and true knowledge of thee, and of thy Son Jesus Christ. Therefore with angels, etc.

Upon *the feast of the Trinity*

Which art one God, one Lord, not one only person, but three persons in one substance; for that which we believe of the glory of the Father, the same we believe of the Son, and of the Holy Ghost, without any difference or inequality. Therefore with angels, etc.

Here follows the prayer that may be said for the whole state of Christ's church:

Almighty and everliving God, which by thy holy Apostle hast taught us to make prayers and supplications, and to give thanks for all men: we humbly beseech thee most mercifully to receive these our prayers, which we offer unto thy divine majesty, beseeching thee to inspire continually the universal church with the spirit of truth, unity and concord; and grant that all they that do confess thy holy name, may agree in the truth of thy holy word, and live in unity and godly love. Specially we beseech thee to save and defend thy servant [*Name*] our king/ queen, that under him/her we may be godly and quietly governed. And grant unto his/her whole counsel, and to all that be put in authority under him/her, that they may truly and indifferently minister justice, to the punishment of wickedness and vice, and to the maintenance of God's true religion and virtue. Give grace, O heavenly Father, to all bishops, pastors, and curates, that they may both by their life and doctrine set forth thy true and lively word, and rightly and duly administer thy holy sacraments. And to all thy people give thy heavenly grace, that with meek heart and due reverence they may hear and receive thy holy word, truly serving thee in holiness and righteousness all the days of their life. And we most humbly beseech thee of thy goodness, O Lord, to comfort and succour all them, which in this transitory life be in trouble, sorrow, need, sickness or any other adversity.

And especially we commend unto thy merciful goodness, this congregation which is here assembled in thy name, to celebrate the commemoration of the most glorious death of thy Son. And here we do give unto thee most high praise, and hearty thanks, for the wonderful grace and virtue, declared in all thy saints, from the beginning of the world; and chiefly in the glorious and most blessed Virgin Mary, mother of thy Son Jesus Christ our Lord and God, and in the holy patriarchs, prophets, apostles and martyrs, whose examples, O Lord, and steadfastness in thy faith, and keeping thy holy commandments, grant us to follow. We commend unto thy mercy, O Lord, all other thy servants, which are departed hence from us, with the sign of faith, and now do rest in the sleep of peace: grant unto them, we beseech thee, thy mercy, and everlasting peace; and that, at the day of the general resurrection, we and all they which are of the mystical body of thy Son, may altogether be set on his right hand, and hear his most joyful voice: Come unto me, O ye that be blessed of my Father, and possess the kingdom, which is prepared for you from the beginning of the world. Grant this, O Father, for Jesus Christ's sake, our only mediator and advocate. **Amen.**

These collects may also be used:

Assist us mercifully, O Lord, in these our supplications and prayers, and dispose the way of thy servants toward the attainment of everlasting salvation, that among all the changes and chances of this mortal life, they may ever be defended by thy most gracious and ready help; through Christ our Lord. **Amen.**

O almighty Lord and everliving God, vouchsafe, we beseech thee, to direct, sanctify and govern both our hearts and bodies, in the ways of thy laws, and in the works of thy commandments, that through thy most mighty protection, both here and ever, we may be pre-served in body and soul; through our Lord and saviour Jesus Christ. **Amen.**

Grant, we beseech thee, almighty God, that the words we have heard this day with our outward ears, may through thy grace be so grafted inwardly in our hearts, that they may bring forth in us the fruit of good living, to the honour and praise of thy name; through Jesus Christ our Lord. **Amen.**

Prevent us, O Lord, in all our doings with thy most gracious favour, and further us with thy continual help, that in all our works begun, continued and ended in thee we may glorify thy holy name, and finally by thy mercy obtain everlasting life; through Jesus Christ our Lord. **Amen.**

Almighty God, the fountain of all wisdom, which knowest our necessities before we ask, and our ignorance in asking, we beseech thee to have compassion upon our infirmities; and those things which for our unworthiness we dare not, and for our blindness we cannot ask, vouchsafe to give us for the worthiness of thy Son, Jesus Christ our Lord. **Amen.**

Almighty God, which hast promised to hear the petitions of them that ask in thy Son's name, we beseech thee mercifully to incline thine ears to us that have made now our prayers and supplications unto thee; and grant that those things which we have faithfully asked according to thy will, may effectually be obtained to the relief of our necessity, and to the setting forth of thy glory; through Jesus Christ our Lord. **Amen.**

BAPTISM

If this takes place at Matins or Evensong, it should start immediately after the last Canticle.

This may be used both for children and for those of riper years.

Minister   Dear beloved, forasmuch as all men are con-
            ceived and born in sin, and that no man born
            in sin can enter into the kingdom of God,
            except he be regenerate, and born anew of
            water and the Holy Ghost, I beseech you to
            call upon God the Father through our Lord
            Jesus Christ, that of his bounteous mercy he
            will grant to this person that thing, which by
            nature s/he cannot have, that is to say, s/he
            may be baptized with the Holy Ghost, and
            received into Christ's holy church, and be
            made a lively member of the same.

Then the minister shall say:

            Almighty and everlasting God, which of thy
            justice didst destroy by floods of water the
            whole world for sin, except eight persons,
            whom of thy mercy the same time thou didst
            save in the ark; and when thou didst drown
            in the Red Sea wicked king Pharaoh with all
            his army, yet, at the same time, thou didst
            lead thy people the children of Israel safely
            through the midst thereof: whereby thou didst

figure the washing of thy holy baptism; and by the baptism of thy well beloved Son Jesus Christ, thou didst sanctify the flood Jordan, and all other waters to this mystical washing away of sin. We beseech thee, for thy infinite mercies, that thou wilt mercifully look upon this person, and sanctify him/her with thy Holy Ghost; that by this wholesome law of regeneration, whatsoever sin is in him/her may be washed clean away, that s/he, being delivered from thy wrath, may be received into the ark of Christ's church, and so saved from perishing; and being fervent in spirit, steadfast in faith, joyful through hope, rooted in charity, may ever serve thee; and finally attain to everlasting life, with all thy holy and chosen people. This grant us we beseech thee, for Jesus Christ's sake our Lord. **Amen.**

Here shall the minister ask what shall be the name of the person to be baptized; and when he has been told the name, then shall he make a cross upon the person's forehead and breast, saying:

[Name], receive the sign of the holy cross, both in thy forehead, and in thy breast, in token that thou shalt not be ashamed to confess thy faith in Christ crucified, and manfully to fight under his banner against sin, the world, and the devil, and to continue his faithful soldier and servant unto thy life's end. **Amen.**

Then the minister, looking upon the person to be baptized, shall say:

I command thee, unclean spirit, in the name of the Father, of the Son, and of the Holy Ghost, that thou come out and depart from this person, whom our Lord Jesus Christ hath vouchsafed to call to his holy baptism, to be a member of his body and of his holy congregation. Therefore, thou cursed spirit, remember thy sentence, remember thy judgement, remember the day is at hand, wherein thou shalt burn in fire everlasting, prepared for thee and thy angels. And presume not hereafter to exercise any tyranny towards this person, whom Christ hath bought with his precious blood, and by this his holy baptism calleth to be of his flock.

Then shall the minister say:

Minister   The Lord be with you.
All   **And with thy spirit.**
Minister   Hear now the gospel written by St John.

The minister, or the person that is appointed, shall read the Gospel, written in the third chapter of the Gospel according to St John, verses one to eight.

There may follow a sermon or homily.

Then shall be said:

Minister   Our Father,

All   **which art in heaven, hallowed be thy name. Thy kingdom come. Thy will be done in earth as it is in heaven. Give us this day our daily bread. And forgive us our trespasses, as we forgive them that trespass against us. And lead us not into temptation, but deliver us from evil. Amen**

The minister shall add also this prayer:

Almighty and everlasting God, heavenly Father, we give thee humble thanks, that thou hast vouchsafed to call us to knowledge of thy grace, and faith in thee: increase and confirm this faith in us evermore; give thy Holy Spirit to this person, that s/he may be born again, and be made an heir of everlasting salvation, through our Lord Jesus Christ; who liveth and reigneth with thee and the Holy Spirit, now and for ever. **Amen.**

Then shall the minister lead the person to be baptized to the font, and say:

The Lord vouchsafe to receive you into his holy household, and to keep and govern you always in the same, that you may have everlasting life. **Amen.**

Then shall the minister demand of the person to be baptized or the parents and godparents presenting him/her, the questions following:

Minister   Do you forsake the devil and all his works?

Answer   I forsake them.

Minister   Do you forsake the vain pomp and glory of the world, with all the covetous desires of the same?

Answer   I forsake them.

Minister   Do you forsake the carnal desires of the flesh, so that thou wilt not follow, nor be led by them?

Answer   I forsake them.

Minister   Do you believe in God the Father almighty, Maker of heaven and earth?

Answer   I believe.

Minister   Do you believe in Jesus Christ his only begotten Son our Lord, and that he was conceived by the Holy Ghost, born of the Virgin Mary, that he suffered under Pontius Pilate, was crucified, dead and buried; that he went down into hell and also did rise again the third day; that he ascended into heaven, and sitteth on the right hand of God the Father almighty; and from thence shall come again at the end of the world, to judge the quick and the dead. Do you believe this?

Answer   I believe.

Minister	Do you believe in the Holy Ghost, the holy catholic church, the communion of saints, remission of sins, resurrection of the flesh, and everlasting life after death?
Answer	**I believe.**
Minister	What do you desire?
Answer	**Baptism.**
Minister	Will you be baptized?
Answer	**I will.**

Then shall the minister take the person, and ask the name. And naming the person, shall dip him/her into the water thrice. First dipping the right side, second the left side; the third time dipping the face toward the font. So it be discreetly and carefully done, saying:

> [Name], I baptize thee in the name of the Father and of the Son and of the Holy Ghost. **Amen.**

Then the minister shall put upon the person baptized a white vesture, and say:

> Take this white vesture for a token of the innocence, which by God's grace in this holy sacrament of baptism, is given unto thee; and for a sign whereby thou art admonished, so long as thou livest, to give thyself to innocence of living, that, after this transitory life, thou mayest be partaker of the life everlasting. **Amen.**

Then the minister shall anoint the person baptized on the head, saying:

> Almighty God, the Father of our Lord Jesus Christ, who hath regenerated thee by water and the Holy Ghost, and hath given unto thee remission of all thy sins: he vouchsafes to anoint thee with the unction of his Holy Spirit, and bring thee to the inheritance of everlasting life. **Amen.**

CONFIRMATION

So soon as people can say the Lord's Prayer, the Ten Commandments, and also can answer to the questions of the Catechism, then shall they be brought to the bishop. And the bishop shall confirm them.

A priest shall say to those to be confirmed, and they shall answer:

Priest   Our help is in the name of the Lord;
Answer   **Which hath made both heaven and earth.**
Priest   Blessed is the name of the Lord;
Answer   **Henceforth world without end.**
Priest   The Lord be with you;
Answer   **And with thy spirit.**

Then the priest shall say:

> Almighty and everlasting God, who hast vouchsafed to regenerate these thy servants of water and the Holy Ghost, and hast given unto them forgiveness of all their sins: send down from heaven we beseech thee, O Lord, upon them thy Holy Ghost the comforter, with the manifold gifts of grace, the spirit of wisdom and understanding; the spirit of counsel and ghostly strength; the spirit of knowledge and true godliness; and fulfil them, O Lord, with the spirit of thy holy fear.
> **Amen.**

Sign them, O Lord, and mark them to be thine for ever, by the virtue of thy holy cross and passion. Confirm and strengthen them with the inward unction of thy Holy Ghost, mercifully unto everlasting life. **Amen.**

Then the Bishop shall cross them in the forehead, and lay his hands upon their heads, saying:

[*Name*], I sign thee with the sign of the cross, and lay my hand upon thee. In the name of the Father, and of the Son, and of the Holy Ghost. Amen.

And thus shall he do to every person one after another. And when he hath laid his hand upon every one, then shall he say and they shall answer:

Bishop   The peace of the Lord abide with you;
Answer   And with thy spirit.

Then the bishop or the priest shall say:

Almighty everliving God, which makest us both to will and to do those things that be good and acceptable unto thy majesty: we make our humble supplications unto thee for these persons, upon whom after the example of thy holy apostles we have laid our hands, to certify them by this sign of thy favour and gracious goodness toward them. Let thy Fatherly hand, we beseech thee, ever be over them; let thy Holy Spirit ever be with them; and so lead them in the knowledge and obedience of thy word, that in the end they may obtain the life everlasting, through our Lord Jesus Christ, who with thee and the Holy Ghost, liveth and reigneth, one God, world without end. **Amen.**

Then shall the bishop bless them, saying:

The blessing of God almighty, the Father, the Son, and the Holy Ghost, be upon you, and remain with you for ever. **Amen.**

MATRIMONY

At the time appointed, the persons to be married shall come into the body of the church, with their friends and neighbours. There may be singing, a gospel and a sermon. Then shall the minister say:

Dearly beloved friends, we are gathered together here in the sight of God, and in the face of his congregation, to join together this man and this woman in holy matrimony, which is an honourable estate instituted of God in paradise, in the time of man's innocence, signifying unto us the mystical union that is betwixt Christ and his church; which holy estate Christ adorned and beautified with his presence and first miracle that he wrought in Cana of Galilee, and is commended of Saint Paul to be honourable among all men; and therefore is not to be enterprised, nor taken in hand unadvisedly, lightly, or wantonly, to satisfy men's carnal lusts and appetites, like brute beasts that have no understanding; but reverently, discreetly, advisedly, soberly, and in the fear of God, duly considering the causes for the which matrimony was ordained.

One cause was the procreation of children, to be brought up in the fear and nurture of the Lord, and praise of God. Secondly it was ordained for a remedy against sin, and to avoid fornication, that such persons as be married might live chastely in matrimony, and keep themselves undefiled members of Christ's body. Thirdly for the mutual society, help and comfort, that the one ought to have of the other, both in prosperity and adversity. Into the which holy estate these two persons present come now to be joined.

Therefore if any man can show any just cause why they may not lawfully be joined so together, let him now speak, or else hereafter for ever hold his peace.

And also speaking to the persons that shall be married, he shall say:

I require and charge you, as you will answer at the dreadful day of judgement when the secrets of all hearts shall be disclosed, that if either of you do know any impediment, why you may not be lawfully joined together in matrimony, that ye confess it. For be ye well assured, that so many as be coupled together otherwise than God's word doth allow, are not joined of God, neither is their matrimony lawful.

If no impediment be alleged, then shall the minister say unto the man:

Minister   [Name], wilt thou have this woman to thy
             wedded wife, to live together after God's
             ordinance in the holy estate of matrimony?
             Wilt thou love her, comfort her, honour, and
             keep her in sickness and in health? And
             forsaking all other keep thee only to her, so
             long as you both shall live?

Man   **I will.**

Then shall the minister say to the woman:

Minister   [Name], wilt thou have this man to thy
             wedded husband, to live together after God's
             ordinance, in the holy estate of matrimony?
             Wilt thou obey him, and serve him, love,
             honour, and keep him in sickness and in
             health? And forsaking all other keep thee only
             to him, so long as you both shall live?

Woman   **I will.**

Minister   Who giveth this woman to be married to this
             man?

And the minister, receiving the woman at her father's
or friend's hands, shall cause the man to take the
woman by the right hand, and so either to give their
troth to the other. The man first saying:

Man   **I [Name] take thee [Name] to my wedded
             wife, to have and to hold from this day
             forward, for better, for worse, for richer,
             for poorer, in sickness, and in health,**

to love and to cherish, till death us do part, according to God's holy ordinance, and thereto I plight thee my troth.

Then shall they loose their hands, and the woman taking again the man by the right hand, shall say:

Woman   I [Name] take thee [Name] to my wedded husband, to have and to hold from this day forward, for better, for worse, for richer, for poorer, in sickness, and in health, to love, cherish, and to obey, till death us do part, according to God's holy ordinance, and thereto I give thee my troth.

Ring(s) shall be handed to the minister. The minister shall offer the ring(s), to be put on the fourth finger of the left hand.

Then these words shall be said:

Man (followed by Woman)

With this ring I thee wed; with my body I thee worship; and with all my worldly goods I thee endow. In the name of the Father, and of the Son, and of the Holy Ghost. Amen.

Then the minister shall say:

O eternal God, creator and preserver of all mankind, giver of all spiritual grace, the author of everlasting life: send thy blessing upon these thy servants, this man, and this woman, whom we bless in thy name, that as Isaac and Rebecca lived faithfully together, so these persons may surely perform and keep the vow and covenant betwixt them made, whereof the ring given, and received, is a token and pledge; and may ever remain in perfect love and peace together, and live according to thy laws; through Jesus Christ our Lord. **Amen.**

Then shall the minister join their hands together, and say:

Those whom God hath joined together, let no man put asunder.

Then shall the minister speak unto the people:

Forasmuch as [Name] and [Name] have consented together in holy wedlock, and have witnessed the same here before God and this company; and thereto have given and pledged their troth either to other, and have declared the same by giving and receiving a ring, and by joining of hands: I pronounce that they be man and wife together. In the name of the Father, of the Son, and of the Holy Ghost. **Amen.**

If no priest is present, the following blessing shall not be said. If a priest is present, he shall add this blessing:

God the Father bless you; God the Son keep you; God the Holy Ghost lighten your understanding. The Lord mercifully with his favour look upon you, and so fill you with all spiritual benediction, and grace, that you may have remission of your sins in this life, and in the world to come life everlasting. **Amen**.

Then shall they go into the choir, while the people sing. The singing ended, and the man and woman kneeling afore the altar, the minister standing at the altar, and turning his face toward them, shall say:

Minister	Lord have mercy upon us.
All	**Christ, have mercy upon us**
Minister	Lord, have mercy upon us.
All	**Our Father, which art in heaven, hallowed be thy name. Thy kingdom come. Thy will be done in earth as it is in heaven. Give us this day our daily bread. And forgive us our trespasses, as we forgive them that trespass against us. And lead us not into temptation, but deliver us from evil. Amen**
Minister	O Lord, save thy servant and thy handmaid;
All	**Which put their trust in thee.**
Minister	O Lord, send them help from thy holy place;
All	**And evermore defend them.**
Minister	Be unto them a tower of strength;
All	**From the face of their enemy.**

Minister	O Lord hear my prayer;
All	**And let my cry come unto thee.**
Minister	Let us pray.

The prayer following shall be omitted when the woman is past childbirth:

O merciful Lord, and heavenly Father, by whose gracious gift mankind is increased: we beseech thee assist with thy blessing these two persons, that they may both be fruitful in procreation of children, and also live together so long in godly love and honesty, that they may see their children's children, unto the third and fourth generation, unto thy praise and honour; through Jesus Christ our Lord. **Amen.**

O God, which by thy mighty power hast made all things of naught, which also after other things set in order didst appoint that out of man, created after thine own image and similitude, woman should take her beginning; and, knitting them together, didst teach, that it should never be lawful to put asunder those, whom thou by matrimony hadst made one; O God, which hast consecrated the state of matrimony to such an excellent mystery, that in it is signified and represented the spiritual marriage and unity betwixt Christ and his church: look mercifully upon these thy servants, that both this man may love his wife, according to thy word, as Christ did love his spouse the church, who gave himself for it, loving and cherishing it even as his own flesh; and also that this woman may be loving and amiable to her husband as Rachel, wise as Rebecca, faithful and obedient as Sarah, and in all quietness, sobriety, and peace, be a follower of holy and godly matrons. O Lord, bless them both, and grant them to inherit thy everlasting kingdom, through Jesus Christ, our Lord. **Amen.**

If there is no priest present, the following blessing shall not be said. If a priest is present, he shall bless the man and the woman:

Almighty God, which at the beginning did create our first parents Adam and Eve, and did sanctify and join them together in marriage: pour upon you the richness of his grace, sanctify and bless you, that you may please him both in body and soul; and live together in holy love unto your lives' end. **Amen.**

The newly married persons may now receive holy communion.

The registration of the marriage may take place now, or at a registry office prior to this service.

VISITATION OF THE SICK

The minister entering into the sick person's house shall say:

> Peace be in this house, and to all that dwell in it.

When he cometh into the sick person's presence, the minister shall say this, and the sick person shall respond:

Minister Remember not, Lord, our iniquities, nor the iniquities of our forefathers. Spare us, good Lord, spare thy people, whom thou hast redeemed with thy most precious blood, and be not angry with us for ever.
Lord, have mercy on us.

Answer **Christ, have mercy on us.**

Minister Lord, have mercy on us.

Both **Our Father, which art in heaven, hallowed be thy name. Thy kingdom come. Thy will be done in earth as it is in heaven. Give us this day our daily bread. And forgive us our trespasses, as we forgive them that trespass against us. And lead us not into temptation, but deliver us from evil. Amen.**

Minister O Lord, save thy servant;

Answer **Put my trust in thee, O Lord.**

Minister Send help from thy holy place;

Answer **And evermore mightily defend me.**

Minister Let the enemy have no advantage;

Answer **Nor the wicked approach to hurt me.**

Minister	Be, O Lord, a strong tower;
Answer	**From the face of my enemy.**
Minister	Lord, hear my prayer;
Answer	**And let my cry come unto thee.**

Then the minister shall say this prayer:

> O Lord, look down from heaven, behold, visit, and release this thy servant. Look upon him/her with the eyes of thy mercy, give him/her comfort, and sure confidence in thee. Defend him/her from the danger of the enemy, and keep him/her in perpetual peace, and safety, through Jesus Christ our Lord. **Amen.**

Here shall the sick person make a special confession, if he/she feels his/her conscience troubled with any weighty matter. After which confession, the priest shall absolve him/her after this form; and the same form of absolution shall be used in all private confessions. If there is no priest present, the absolution shall not be said.

> O Lord Jesus Christ, who hath left power to his church to absolve all sinners, which truly repent and believe in him: of his great mercy forgive thee thine offences; and by his authority committed to me, I absolve thee from all thy sins, in the name of the Father, and of the Son, and of the Holy Ghost. **Amen.**

And then the minister shall say the collect following:

O most merciful God, which according to the
multitude of thy mercies, dost so put away
the sins of those which truly repent, that thou
rememberest them no more: open thy eye of
mercy upon this thy servant, who most
earnestly desireth pardon and forgiveness;
renew in him/her, most loving Father, whatsoever hath been decayed by the fraud and
malice of the devil, or by his/her own carnal
will and frailness; preserve and continue this
sick member in the unity of thy church,
consider his/her contrition, accept his/her
tears, assuage his pain, as shall be seen to thee
most expedient for him/her. And forasmuch
as he/she putteth his/her full trust only in thy
mercy; impute not unto him/her his/her
former sins, but take him/her unto thy
favour; through the merits of thy most dearly
beloved Son Jesus Christ. **Amen.**

And the minister shall add this anthem:

O saviour of the world, save us, which by thy
cross and precious blood hast redeemed us;
help us, we beseech thee, O God.

Then shall the minister say to the sick person:

> The almighty Lord, which is a most strong tower to all them that put their trust in him, to whom all things in heaven, in earth, and under earth, do bow and obey: be now and evermore thy defence, and make thee know and feel, that there is no other name under heaven given to man, in whom and through whom thou mayest receive health and salvation, but only the name of our Lord Jesus Christ. **Amen.**

Then shall the minister anoint the sick person upon the forehead or the breast, making the sign of the cross, saying thus:

> As with this visible oil thy body outwardly is anointed; so our heavenly Father almighty God, grant of his infinite goodness, that thy soul inwardly may be anointed with the Holy Ghost, who is the spirit of all strength, comfort, relief and gladness. And vouchsafe for his great mercy, if it be his blessed will to restore unto thee thy bodily health and strength, to serve him, and send thee release of all thy pains, troubles, and diseases, both in body and mind. And howsoever his goodness, by his divine and unsearchable providence, shall dispose of thee; we, his unworthy ministers and servants, humbly beseech thy

eternal majesty, to do with thee according to
the multitude of his innumerable mercies, and
to pardon thee all thy sins and offences, committed by all thy bodily senses, passions, and
carnal affections; who also vouchsafe mercifully to grant unto thee ghostly strength, by
his Holy Spirit, to withstand and overcome all
temptations and assaults of thine adversary,
that in no wise he prevail against thee, but
that thou mayest have perfect victory and
triumph against the devil, sin, and death,
through Christ our Lord; who by his death
hath overcome the prince of death, and with
the Father, and the Holy Ghost evermore
liveth and reigneth God, world without end.
Amen.

At the previous celebration of the Holy Communion in
the church, the priest shall reserve so much of the
sacrament of the body and blood as shall serve sick
persons. After distributing Communion the minister
shall say the Collect:

Almighty and everliving God, we most
heartily thank thee, for that thou hast vouchsafed to feed us in these holy mysteries, with
the spiritual food of the most precious body
and blood of thy Son, our saviour Jesus
Christ, and hast assured us, duly receiving the
same, of thy favour and goodness toward us,

and that we are very members incorporate in thy mystical body, which is the blessed company of all faithful people, and heirs through hope of thy everlasting kingdom, by the merits of the most previous death and passion of thy dear Son. We therefore most humbly beseech thee, O heavenly Father, so to assist us with thy grace, that we may continue in that holy fellowship, and do all such good works, as thou hast prepared for us to walk in; through Jesus Christ our Lord, to whom with thee and the Holy Ghost, be all honour and glory, world without end. **Amen.**

BURIAL OF THE DEAD

The minister meeting the corpse shall say:

I am the resurrection and the life, saith the Lord; he that believeth in me, yea though he were dead, yet shall he live. And whosoever liveth and believeth in me shall not die for ever.

I know that my redeemer liveth, and that I shall rise out of the earth on the last day, and shall be covered again with my skin and shall see God in my flesh; yea and I myself shall behold him, not with other but with these same eyes.

We brought nothing into this world, neither may we carry anything out of this world. The Lord giveth, and the Lord taketh away. Even as it pleaseth the Lord, so cometh things to pass; blessed be the name of the Lord.

Then shall follow the lesson, which may be taken out of the fifteenth chapter of the First Epistle to the Corinthians.

Then may follow a sermon.

The lesson and sermon ended, then the minister shall say:

Minister   Lord, have mercy upon us.

All   Christ, have mercy upon us.

Minister   Lord, have mercy upon us.

All	**Our Father, which art in heaven, hallowed be thy name. Thy kingdom come. Thy will be done in earth as it is in heaven. Give us this day our daily bread. And forgive us our trespasses, as we forgive them that trespass against us. And lead us not into temptation, but deliver us from evil. Amen**
Minister	Enter not, O Lord, into judgement with thy servant;
All	**For in thy sight no living creature shall be justified.**
Minister	From the gates of hell;
All	**Deliver their souls, O Lord.**
Minister	I believe to see the goodness of the Lord;
All	**In the land of the living.**
Minister	O Lord, graciously hear my prayer;
All	**And let my cry come unto thee.**
Minister	O Lord, with whom do live the spirits of them that be dead; and in whom the souls of them that be elected, after they be delivered from the burden of the flesh, are in joy and felicity: grant unto this thy servant, that the sins which he/she committed in this world be not imputed unto him/her, but that he/she, escaping the gates of hell and pains of eternal darkness, may ever dwell in the region of light, with Abraham, Isaac, and Jacob, in the place where is no weeping, sorrow, nor heaviness; and when that dreadful day of the

general resurrection shall come, make him/her
to rise also with the just and righteous, and
receive this body again to glory, then made
pure and incorruptible. Set him/her on the
right hand of thy Son Jesus Christ, among thy
holy and elect, that then he/she may hear
with them these most sweet and comfortable
words: Come to me ye blessed of my Father,
possess the kingdom which hath been
prepared for you from the beginning of the
world. Grant this we beseech thee, O merciful
Father, through Jesus Christ our mediator and
redeemer. **Amen.**

Then shall be said this collect:

O Merciful God, the Father of our Lord Jesus
Christ, who is the resurrection and the life, in
whom whosoever believeth shall live though
he die, and whosoever liveth, and believeth in
him shall not die eternally; who also hath
taught us by his holy Apostle Paul not to be
sorry as men without hope for them that sleep
in him: we meekly beseech thee, O Father, to
raise us from the death of sin, unto the life of
righteousness, that when we shall depart this
life, we may sleep in him, as our hope is this
our brother/sister doeth, and at the general
resurrection in the last day, both we and this
our brother/sister departed, receiving again

our bodies, and rising again in thy most gracious favour, may with all thine elect saints, obtain eternal joy. Grant this, O Lord God, by the means of our advocate Jesus Christ, which with thee and the Holy Ghost, liveth and reigneth one God for ever. **Amen.**

When the corpse is committed, the minister shall say:

Man is born of a woman, hath but a short time to live, and is full of misery; he cometh up and is cut down like a flower; he flieth as it were a shadow, and never continueth in one state.

In the midst of life we be in death. Of whom may we seek for succour but of thee, O Lord, which for our sins justly art moved? Yet, O Lord God most holy, O Lord most mighty, O holy and most merciful saviour, deliver us not into the bitter pains of eternal death. Thou knowest, Lord, the secrets of our hearts: shut not up thy merciful eyes to our prayers. But spare us, Lord most holy, O God most mighty, O holy and merciful saviour, thou most worthy judge eternal, suffer us not at our last hour for any pains of death to fall from thee.

Then the minister shall say:

> I commend thy soul to God the Father
> almighty, and thy body to the ground, earth
> to earth, ashes to ashes, dust to dust, in sure
> and certain hope of resurrection to eternal life
> through our Lord Jesus Christ, who shall
> change our vile body, that it may be like to
> his glorious body, according to the mighty
> working whereby he is able to subdue all
> things to himself.

Then shall be said:

> I have heard a voice from heaven saying, unto
> me: Write, blessed are the dead which die in
> the Lord. Even so saith the Spirit, that they
> rest from their labours.

Then the following prayers shall be said:

> We commend unto thy hands of mercy, most
> merciful Father, the soul of this our departed
> brother/sister [Name]. And his/her body we
> commit to the earth, beseeching thine infinite
> goodness, to give us grace to live in thy fear
> and love, and to die in thy favour; that when
> the judgement shall come which thou hast
> committed to thy well beloved Son, both this
> our brother/sister, and we, may be found
> acceptable in thy sight, and receive that
> blessing, which thy well beloved Son shall

then pronounce to all that love and fear thee, saying: Come ye blessed children of my Father; receive the kingdom prepared for you before the beginning of the world. Grant this, merciful Father, for the honour of Jesus Christ, our only saviour, mediator, and advocate. **Amen.**

Almighty God, we give thee hearty thanks for this thy servant, whom thou hast delivered from the miseries of this wretched world, from the body of death and all temptation. And, as we trust, hast brought his/her soul which he committed into thy holy hands, into sure consolation and rest. Grant we beseech thee, that at the day of judgement, his/her soul and all the souls of thy elect, departed out of this life, may with us and we with them, fully receive thy promises, and be made perfect altogether through the glorious resurrection of thy Son Jesus Christ our Lord. **Amen.**

THE LITANY

Minister	O God the Father of heaven : have mercy upon us miserable sinners.
All	**O God the Father of heaven : have mercy upon us miserable sinners.**
Minister	O God the Son, redeemer of the world : have mercy upon us miserable sinners.
All	**O God the Son, redeemer of the world : have mercy upon us miserable sinners.**
Minister	O God the Holy Ghost, proceeding from the Father and the Son : have mercy upon us miserable sinners.
All	**O God the Holy Ghost, proceeding from the Father and the Son : have mercy upon us miserable sinners.**
Minister	O holy, blessed and glorious Trinity, three persons and one God : have mercy upon us miserable sinners.
All	**O holy, blessed and glorious Trinity, three persons and one God : have mercy upon us miserable sinners.**
Minister	Remember not Lord, our offences, nor the offences of our forefathers, neither take thou vengeance of our sins : spare us good Lord, spare thy people, whom thou hast redeemed with thy most precious blood, and be not angry with us for ever.
All	**Spare us, good Lord.**

Minister	From all evil and mischief, from sin, from the crafty assaults of the devil, from thy wrath, and from everlasting damnation:
All	**Good Lord, deliver us.**
Minister	From blindness of heart, from pride, vain-glory, and hypocrisy, from ennui, hatred and malice, and all uncharitableness:
All	**Good Lord, deliver us.**
Minister	From fornication and all other deadly sin, and from all the deceits of the world, the flesh and the devil:
All	**Good Lord, deliver us.**
Minister	From lightning and tempest, from plague, pestilence and famine, from battle and murder, and from sudden death:
All	**Good Lord, deliver us.**
Minister	From all sedition and privy conspiracy, from all false doctrine and heresy, from hardness of heart, and contempt of thy word and commandments:
All	**Good Lord, deliver us.**
Minister	By the mystery of thy holy incarnation, by thy holy nativity and circumcision, by thy baptism, fasting and temptation:
All	**Good Lord, deliver us.**
Minister	By thine agony and bloody sweat, by thy cross and passion, by thy precious death and burial, by thy glorious resurrection and ascension, by the coming of the Holy Ghost:

All **Good Lord, deliver us.**

Minister In all time of our tribulation, in all time of our wealth, in the hour of death, in the day of judgement:

All **Good Lord, deliver us.**

Minister We sinners do beseech thee to hear us, O Lord God, and that it may please thee to rule and govern thy holy church universal in the right way:

All **We beseech thee to hear us good Lord.**

Minister That it may please thee to keep [Name], thy servant, our king/queen and governor:

All **We beseech thee to hear us good Lord.**

Minister That it may please thee to rule her heart in thy faith, fear and love, that she may always have affiance in thee, and ever seek thy honour and glory:

All **We beseech thee to hear us good Lord.**

Minister That it may please thee to be her defender and keeper, giving her the victory over all her enemies:

All **We beseech thee to hear us good Lord.**

Minister That it may please thee to illuminate all bishops, pastors and ministers of the church, with true knowledge and understanding of thy word, and that both by their preaching and living they may set it forth, and show it accordingly:

All **We beseech thee to hear us good Lord.**

Minister	That it may please thee to endue the lords of the council and all the nobility, with grace, wisdom and understanding:
All	**We beseech thee to hear us good Lord.**
Minister	That it may please thee to bless and keep the magistrates, giving them grace to execute justice, and to maintain truth:
All	**We beseech thee to hear us good Lord.**
Minister	That it may please them to bless and keep all thy people:
All	**We beseech thee to hear us good Lord.**
Minister	That it may please thee to give to all nations unity, peace and concord:
All	**We beseech thee to hear us good Lord.**
Minister	That it may please thee to give us an heart to love and dread thee, and diligently to live after thy commandments:
All	**We beseech thee to hear us good Lord.**
Minister	That it may please thee to give all thy people increase of grace, to hear meekly thy word, and to receive it with pure affection, and to bring forth the fruits of the Spirit:
All	**We beseech thee to hear us good Lord.**
Minister	That it may please thee to bring into the way of truth all such as have erred and are deceived:
All	**We beseech thee to hear us good Lord.**

Minister	That it may please thee to strengthen such as do stand, and to comfort and help the weak-hearted, and to raise up them that fall, and finally to beat down Satan under our feet:
All	**We beseech thee to hear us good Lord.**
Minister	That it may please thee to succour, help and comfort all that be in danger, necessity and tribulation:
All	**We beseech thee to hear us good Lord.**
Minister	That it may please thee to preserve all that travel by land or by water, all women labouring of child, all sick persons, and young children, and to show thy pity upon all prisoners and captives:
All	**We beseech thee to hear us good Lord.**
Minister	That it may please thee to defend and provide for the fatherless children and widows, and all that be desolate and oppressed:
All	**We beseech thee to hear us good Lord.**
Minister	That it may please thee to have mercy upon all men:
All	**We beseech thee to hear us good Lord.**
Minister	That it may please thee to forgive our enemies, persecutors and slanderers, and to turn their hearts:
All	**We beseech thee to hear us good Lord.**
Minister	That it may please thee to give and preserve to our use the kindly fruits of the earth, so as in due time we may enjoy them:
All	**We beseech thee to hear us good Lord.**

Minister	That it may please thee to give us true repentance, to forgive us all our sins, negligences, and ignorances, and to endue us with the grace of thy Holy Spirit to amend our lives according to thy holy word:
All	**We beseech thee to hear us good Lord.**
Minister	Son of God, we beseech thee to hear us.
All	**Son of God, we beseech thee to hear us.**
Minister	O lamb of God, that takest away the sins of the world:
All	**Have mercy upon us.**
Minister	O Christ hear us.
All	**O Christ hear us.**
Minister	Lord have mercy upon us.
All	**Lord have mercy upon us.**
Minister	Christ have mercy upon us.
All	**Christ have mercy upon us**
Minister	Lord have mercy upon us.
All	**Lord have mercy upon us.**
	Our Father, which art in heaven, hallowed be thy name. Thy kingdom come. Thy will be done in earth as it is in heaven. Give us this day our daily bread. And forgive us our trespasses, as we forgive them that trespass against us. And lead us not into temptation, but deliver us from evil. Amen
Minister	O Lord, deal not with us after our sins.
All	**Neither reward us after our iniquities.**
Minister	Let us pray:

O God, merciful Father, that despisest not the sighing of a contrite heart, nor the desire of such as be sorrowful, mercifully assist our prayers that we make before thee in all our troubles and adversities, whensoever they oppress us; and graciously hear us, that those evils, which the craft and subtleties of the devil or man worketh against us, be brought to nought, and by the providence of thy goodness, they may be dispersed, that we thy servants, being hurt by no persecutions, may evermore give thanks unto thee, in thy holy church, through Jesus Christ our Lord.

All   **O Lord, arise, help us, and deliver us for thy name's sake.**

Minister   O God, we have heard with our ears, and our fathers have declared unto us the noble works that thou didst in their days, and in the old time before them.

All   **O Lord, arise, help us, and deliver us for thine honour.**

Minister   Glory be to the Father, the Son, and to the Holy Ghost, as it was in the beginning, is now, and ever shall be, world without end. **Amen.**

Minister   From our enemies defend us, O Christ;

All   **Graciously look upon our afflictions.**

Minister   Pitifully behold the sorrows of our heart;

All   **Mercifully forgive the sins of thy people.**

Minister	Favourably with mercy hear our prayers;
All	**O Son of David, have mercy upon us.**
Minister	Both now and ever vouchsafe to hear us, O Christ.
All	**Graciously hear us, O Christ; graciously hear us, O Lord Christ.**
Minister	O Lord, let thy mercy be showed upon us.
All	**As we do put our trust in thee.**
Minister	Let us pray.

We humbly beseech thee, O Father, mercifully to look upon our infirmities, and for the glory of thy name's sake, turn from us all those evils that we most righteously have deserved; and grant that in all our troubles we may put our whole trust and confidence in thy mercy, and evermore serve thee in pureness of living, to thy honour and glory: through our only mediator and advocate, Jesus Christ our Lord. **Amen.**

Almighty God, which hast given us grace at this time with one accord to make our common supplications unto thee, and dost promise that when two or three be gathered in thy name, thou wilt grant their requests: fulfill now, O Lord, the desires and petitions of thy servants, as may be most expedient for them, granting us in this world knowledge of thy truth, and in the world to come, life ever-lasting. **Amen.**

CATECHISM

This is an instruction to be learned by all people, before they be brought to be confirmed by the bishop.

Question   What is your name?

Answer   **[Name]**

Question   Who gave you this name?

Answer   **My godfathers and godmothers in my baptism, wherein I was made a member of Christ, the child of God and inheritor of the kingdom of heaven.**

Question   What did your godfathers and godmothers then for you?

Answer   **They did promise and vow three things in my name. First, that I should forsake the devil and all his works and pomps, the vanities of the wicked world, and all the sinful lusts of the flesh. Secondly, that I should believe all the articles of the Christian faith. And thirdly, that I should keep God's holy will and commandments and walk in the same all the days of my life.**

Question   Dost thou not think that thou art bound to believe, and to do as they have promised for thee?

Answer   **Yes, verily. And by God's help so I will. And I heartily thank our heavenly Father, that he hath called me to this state of salvation, through Jesus Christ our saviour.**

And I pray God to give me his grace, that I may continue in the same unto my life's end.

Question   Rehearse the articles of thy belief.

Answer   I believe in God the Father almighty, maker of heaven and earth. And in Jesus Christ his only Son our Lord. Which was conceived by the Holy Ghost, born of the Virgin Mary, suffered under Pontius Pilate, was crucified, dead and buried. He descended into hell. The third day he rose again from the dead. He ascended into heaven, and sitteth on the right hand of God the Father almighty. From thence shall he come to judge the quick and the dead. I believe in the Holy Ghost; the holy catholic church; the communion of saints; the forgiveness of sins; the resurrection of the body; and the life everlasting. Amen.

Question   What dost thou chiefly learn in these articles of thy belief?

Answer   First, I learn to believe in God the Father, who hath made me and all the world. Secondly, in God the Son, who hath redeemed me and all mankind. Thirdly, in God the Holy Ghost, who sanctified me and all the elect people of God.

Question You said that your godfathers and godmothers did promise for you that ye should keep God's commandments. Tell me how many there be.

Answer **Ten.**

Question Which be they?

Answer
  i **Thou shalt have none other Gods but me.**

  ii **Thou shalt not make to thyself any graven image, nor the likeness of any thing that is in heaven above, or in the earth beneath, nor in the water under the earth; thou shalt not bow down to them, nor worship them.**

  iii **Thou shalt not take the name of the Lord thy God in vain.**

  iv **Remember that thou keep holy the sabbath day.**

  v **Honour thy father and thy mother.**

  vi **Thou shalt do no murder.**

  vii **Thou shalt not commit adultery.**

  viii **Thou shalt not steal.**

  ix **Thou shalt not bear false witness against thy neighbour.**

  x **Thou shalt not covet thy neighbour's wife, nor his servant, nor his maid, nor his ox, nor his ass, nor any thing that is his.**

Question   What dost thou chiefly learn by these
            commandments?

Answer **I learn two things: my duty towards God,
            and my duty towards my neighbour.**

Question   What is thy duty towards God?

Answer **My duty towards God is, to belong in him;
            to fear him; and to love him with all my
            heart, with all my mind, with all my soul,
            and with all my strength; to worship him;
            to give him thanks; to put my whole trust
            in him; to call upon him; to honour his
            holy name and his word; and to serve him
            truly all the days of my life.**

Question   What is thy duty towards thy neighbour?

Answer **My duty towards my neighbour, is to love
            him as myself; and to do to all men as I
            would they should do to me; to love,
            honour, and succour my father and mother;
            to honour and obey the king/queen and
            his/her ministers; to submit myself to all
            my governors, teachers, spiritual pastors,
            and masters; to order myself lowly and
            reverentially to all my betters; to hurt no
            body by word nor deed; to be true and just
            in all my dealing; to bear no malice nor
            hatred in my heart; to keep my hands from
            picking and stealing, and my tongue from
            evil speaking, lying and slandering; to keep
            my body in temperance, soberness, and**

chastity; not to covet nor desire other men's goods; but learn and labour truly to get my own living, and to do my duty in that state of life, unto which it shall please God to call me.

Question Know this, that thou art not able to do these things of thyself, nor to walk in the commandments of God and to serve him, without his special grace, which thou must learn at all times to call for by diligent prayer. Let me hear therefore if thou canst say the Lord's prayer.

Answer **Our Father, which art in heaven, hallowed be thy name. Thy kingdom come. Thy will be done in earth as it is in heaven. Give us this day our daily bread. And forgive us our trespasses, as we forgive them that trespass against us. And lead us not into temptation, but deliver us from evil. Amen.**

Question What desirest thou of God in this prayer?

Answer **I desire my Lord God our heavenly Father, who is the giver of all goodness, to send his grace unto me, and to all people that we may worship him, serve him, and obey him, as we ought to do. And I pray unto God, that he will send us all things that be needful both for our souls and bodies; and that he will be merciful unto us, and forgive us our sins; and that it will please him**

to save and defend us in all dangers ghostly
and bodily; and that he will keep us from
all sin and wickedness, and from our
ghostly enemy, and from everlasting death.
And this I trust he will do of his mercy and
goodness, through our Lord Jesu Christ.
And therefore I say, Amen. So be it.

COLLECTS, EPISTLES AND GOSPELS

The collects are to be used at Matins, Evensong and Holy Communion throughout the year. The Epistles and Gospels are to be used at Holy Communion.

THE FIRST SUNDAY IN ADVENT

The Collect
Almighty God, give us grace, that we may cast away the works of darkness, and put upon us the armour of light, now in the time of this mortal life, in which thy Son Jesus Christ came to visit us in great humility; that in the last day, when he shall come again in his glorious majesty to judge both the quick and the dead, we may rise to the life immortal, through him who liveth and reigneth with thee and the Holy Ghost, now and ever. **Amen.**

The Epistle
Romans 13.8–14

The Gospel
Matthew 21.1–13

THE SECOND SUNDAY IN ADVENT

The Collect
Blessed Lord, which hast caused all holy Scriptures to be written for our learning, grant us that we may in such wise hear them, read, mark, learn and inwardly digest them; that by patience and comfort of thy holy word, we may embrace and ever hold fast the blessed hope of everlasting life, which thou hast given us in our saviour Jesus Christ. **Amen.**

The Epistle
Romans 15.4–13

The Gospel
Luke 21.25–33

THE THIRD SUNDAY IN ADVENT

The Collect
Lord, we beseech thee, give ear to our prayers, and by thy gracious visitation lighten the darkness of our heart, by our Lord Jesus Christ. **Amen.**

The Epistle
1 Corinthians 4.1–5

The Gospel
Matthew 11.2–10

THE FOURTH SUNDAY IN ADVENT

The Collect
Lord, raise up, we pray thee, thy power, and come among us, and with great might succour us; that whereas, through our sins and wickedness, we are sore let and hindered, thy bountiful grace and mercy, through the satisfaction of thy Son our Lord, may speedily deliver us; to whom with thee and the Holy Ghost be honour and glory, world without end. **Amen.**

| *The Epistle* | *The Gospel* |
| Philippians 4.4–7 | John 1.19–28 |

CHRISTMAS EVE

The Collect
God, which makest us glad with the yearly remembrance of the birth of thy only son Jesus Christ: grant that as we joyfully receive him for our redeemer, so we may with sure confidence behold him, when he shall come to be our judge, who liveth and reigneth with thee and the Holy Ghost, now and ever. **Amen.**

| *The Epistle* | *The Gospel* |
| Titus 2.11–15 | Luke 2.1–14 |

CHRISTMAS DAY
25 DECEMBER

The Collect
Almighty God, which hast given us thy only-begotten
Son to take our nature upon him, and this day to be
born of a pure Virgin, grant that we being regenerate,
and made thy children by adoption and grace, may daily
be renewed by thy Holy Spirit, through the same our
Lord Jesus Christ who liveth and reigneth with thee and
the Holy Ghost, now and ever. **Amen.**

The Epistle   The Gospel
Hebrews 1.1–12   John 1.1–14

ST STEPHEN'S DAY
26 DECEMBER

The Collect
Grant us, O Lord, to learn to love our enemies, by the
example of thy martyr Saint Stephen, who prayed to thee
for his persecutors; which livest and reignest with thee
and the Holy Ghost, now and ever. **Amen.**

The Epistle   The Gospel
Acts 7.55–60   Matthew 23.34–39

ST JOHN THE EVANGELIST'S DAY
27 DECEMBER

The Collect
Merciful Lord, we beseech thee to cast thy bright beams
of light upon thy church, that it being lightened by the
doctrine of thy blessed Apostle and Evangelist John may
attain to thy everlasting gifts; through Jesus Christ our
Lord. **Amen.**

The Epistle
1 John.1–10

The Gospel
John 21.19–25

THE INNOCENTS DAY
28 DECEMBER

The Collect
Almighty God, whose prayers this day the young
innocents thy witnesses hath confessed and shewed forth,
not in speaking but in dying: mortify and kill all vices in
us, that in our conversation our life may express thy
faith, which with our tongues we do confess; through
Jesus Christ our Lord. **Amen.**

The Epistle
Revelation 14.1–5

The Gospel
Matthew 2.13–18

THE SUNDAY AFTER CHRISTMAS DAY

The Collect
Almighty God, which hast given us thy only-begotten
Son to take our nature upon him, and this day to be
born of a pure Virgin, grant that we being regenerate,
and made thy children by adoption and grace, may daily
be renewed by thy Holy Spirit, through the same our
Lord Jesus Christ who liveth and reigneth with thee and
the Holy Ghost, now and ever. **Amen.**

The Epistle
Revelation 21.1–17

The Gospel
Matthew 1.18–25

THE CIRCUMCISION OF CHRIST
1 JANUARY

The Collect
Almighty God, which madest thy blessed Son to be
circumcised, and obedient to the law for man: grant us
the true circumcision of thy spirit, that our hearts, and all
our members, being mortified from all worldly and
carnal lusts, may in all things obey thy blessed will;
through the same thy Son Jesus Christ our Lord. **Amen.**

The Epistle
Romans 4.7–14

The Gospel
Luke 2.15–21

THE EPIPHANY
6 JANUARY

The Collect
O God, which by the leading of a star didst manifest thy
only-begotten Son to the gentiles: mercifully grant, that
we, which know thee now by faith, may after this life
have the fruition of thy glorious godhead; through Christ
our Lord. **Amen.**

The Epistle	*The Gospel*
Ephesians 3.1–12	Matthew 2.1–12

THE FIRST SUNDAY AFTER THE EPIPHANY

The Collect
Lord, we beseech thee mercifully to receive the praises of
thy people which call upon thee; and grant that they may
both perceive and know what things they ought to do,
and also have grace and power faithfully to fulfill the
same. **Amen.**

The Epistle	*The Gospel*
Romans 12.1–5	Luke 2.41–52

THE SECOND SUNDAY AFTER THE EPIPHANY

The Collect
Almighty and everlasting God, which dost govern all things in heaven and earth: mercifully hear the supplications of thy people, and grant us thy peace all the days of our life. **Amen.**

The Epistle	*The Gospel*
Romans 12.6–16	John 2.1–11

THE THIRD SUNDAY AFTER THE EPIPHANY

The Collect
Almighty and everlasting God, mercifully look upon our infirmities, and in all our dangers and necessities, stretch forth thy right hand to help and defend us; through Christ our Lord. **Amen.**

The Epistle	*The Gospel*
Romans 12.17–21	Matthew 8.1–13

THE FOURTH SUNDAY AFTER THE EPIPHANY

The Collect
God, which knowest us to be set in the midst of so
many and great dangers, that for man's frailness we
cannot always stand uprightly; grant to us the health of
body and soul, that all those things which we suffer for
sin, by thy help we may well pass and overcome;
through Christ our Lord. **Amen.**

The Epistle   The Gospel
Romans 13.1–7   Matthew 8.23–34

THE FIFTH SUNDAY AFTER THE EPIPHANY

The Collect
Lord, we beseech thee to keep thy church and household
continually in thy true religion; that they which do lean
only upon hope of thy heavenly grace may evermore be
defended by thy mighty power; through Christ our Lord.
Amen.

The Epistle   The Gospel
Colossians 3.12–17   Matthew 13.24–30

THE SUNDAY CALLED SEPTUAGESIMA

The Collect
O Lord, we beseech thee favourably to hear the prayers
of thy people; that we which are justly punished for our
offences, may be mercifully delivered by thy goodness,
for the glory of thy name, through Jesus Christ our
saviour, who liveth and reigneth with thee and the Holy
Ghost, now and ever. **Amen.**

The Epistle   *The Gospel*
1 Corinthians 9.24–27   Matthew 20.1–16

THE SUNDAY CALLED SEXAGESIMA

The Collect
Lord God, which seest that we put not our trust in any
thing that we do: mercifully grant that by thy power we
may be defended against all adversity; through Jesus
Christ our Lord. **Amen.**

The Epistle   *The Gospel*
2 Corinthians 11.19–31   Luke 8.4–15

THE SUNDAY CALLED QUINQUAGESIMA

The Collect
O Lord, which dost teach us that all our doings without
charity are nothing worth: send thy Holy Ghost, and
pour into our hearts that most excellent gift of charity,
the very bond of peace and all virtues, without the which
whosoever liveth is counted dead before thee; grant this
for thy only Son, Jesus Christ's sake. **Amen.**

The Epistle   The Gospel
1 Corinthians 13.1–13   Luke 18.31–43

ASH WEDNESDAY

The Collect
Almighty and everlasting God, which hatest nothing that
thou hast made, and dost forgive the sins of all them that
be penitent: create and make in us new and contrite
hearts, that we worthily lamenting our sins, and acknow-
ledging our wretchedness, may obtain of thee, the God
of all mercy, perfect remission and forgiveness; through
Jesus Christ our Lord. **Amen.**

The Epistle   The Gospel
1 Corinthians 9.24–27   Matthew 6.16–21

THE FIRST SUNDAY IN LENT

The Collect
O Lord, which for our sake didst fast forty days and forty
nights: give us grace to use such abstinence that, our
flesh being subdued to the spirit, we may ever obey thy
godly motions in righteousness and true holiness, to thy
honour and glory, which livest and reignest with thee
and the Holy Ghost, now and ever. **Amen.**

The Epistle   *The Gospel*
2 Corinthians 6.1–10   Matthew 4.1–11

THE SECOND SUNDAY IN LENT

The Collect
Almighty God, which dost see that we have no power of
ourselves to help ourselves: keep thou us both outwardly
in our bodies, and inwardly in our souls, that we may be
defended from all adversities which may happen to the
body, and from all evil thoughts which may assault and
hurt the soul; through Jesus Christ our Lord. **Amen.**

The Epistle   *The Gospel*
1 Thessalonians 4.1–8   Matthew 15.21–28

THE THIRD SUNDAY IN LENT

The Collect
We beseech thee, almighty God, look upon the hearty desires of thy humble servants, and stretch forth the right hand of thy majesty, to be our defence against all our enemies, through Jesus Christ our Lord. **Amen.**

The Epistle   The Gospel
Ephesians 5.1–14   Luke 11.14–28

THE FOURTH SUNDAY IN LENT

The Collect
Grant, we beseech thee, almighty God, that we, which for our evil deeds are worthily punished, by the comfort of thy grace may mercifully be relieved; through our Lord Jesus Christ. **Amen.**

The Epistle   The Gospel
Galatians 4.21–31   John 6.1–14

THE FIFTH SUNDAY IN LENT

The Collect
We beseech thee, almighty God, mercifully to look upon thy people; that by thy great goodness they may be governed and preserved evermore, both in body and soul; through Jesus Christ our Lord. **Amen.**

The Epistle
Hebrews 9.11–15

The Gospel
John 8.46–59

PALM SUNDAY

The Collect
Almighty and everlasting God, which of thy tender love towards man hast sent our saviour Jesus Christ, to take upon him our flesh, and to suffer death upon the cross, that all mankind should follow the example of his great humility: mercifully grant that we both follow the example of his patience, and be made partakers of his resurrection; through the same Jesus Christ our Lord. **Amen.**

The Epistle
Philippians 2.5–11

The Gospel
Matthew 21.1–11

MAUNDY THURSDAY

The Collect
Almighty and everlasting God, by whose Spirit the whole
body of the church is governed and sanctified: receive
our supplications and prayers, which we offer before thee
for all estates of men in thy holy congregations, that
every member of the same, in his vocation and ministry,
may truly and godly serve thee; through our Lord Jesus
Christ. **Amen.**

The Epistle   The Gospel
1 Corinthians 11.23–28   John 13.1–15

GOOD FRIDAY

The Collect
Almighty God, we beseech thee graciously to behold this
thy family, for which our Lord Jesus Christ was contented
to be betrayed, and given up into the hands of wicked
men, and to suffer death upon the cross; who liveth and
reigneth with thee and the Holy Ghost, now and ever.
Amen.

The Epistle   The Gospel
Hebrew 10.1–10   John 19.1–31

EASTER EVE

The Collect
Almighty and everlasting God, which of thy tender love towards man hast sent our saviour Jesus Christ, to take upon him our flesh, and to suffer death upon the cross, that all mankind should follow the example of his great humility: mercifully grant that we both follow the example of his patience, and be made partakers of his resurrection; through the same Jesus Christ our Lord. **Amen.**

The Epistle
1 Peter 3.17–22

The Gospel
Matthew 27.57–66

EASTER DAY

The minister shall begin the service with the Easter Anthems:

Christ rising again from the dead, now dieth not. Death from henceforth hath no power upon him. For in that he died, he died but once to put away sin; but in that he liveth, he liveth unto God. And so likewise, count yourselves dead unto sin, but living unto God in Christ Jesus our Lord. Alleluya, Alleluya.

Christ is risen again, the first fruits of them that sleep.
For seeing that by man came death; by man also cometh
the resurrection of the dead. For as by Adam all men do
die, so by Christ all men shall be restored to life. Alleluya.

Minister   Shew forth to all nations the glory of God.
Answer   **And among all people his wonderful works;**
Minister   Let us pray.
           O God, who for our redemption didst give
           thine only begotten Son to the death of the
           cross, and by his glorious resurrection hast
           delivered us from the power of our enemy:
           grant us so to die daily from sin, that we may
           evermore live with him in the joy of his
           resurrection; through the same Christ our
           Lord. **Amen.**

The Collect
Almighty God, which through thy only begotten Son
Jesus Christ has overcome death, and opened unto us the
gate of everlasting life: we humbly beseech thee, that as
by thy special grace preventing us thou dost put in our
minds good desires, so by thy continual help we may
bring the same to good effect; through Jesus Christ our
Lord who liveth and reigneth, with thee and the Holy
Ghost, now and ever. **Amen.**

The Epistle   *The Gospel*
1 Corinthians 5.7–8   Mark 16.1–8

THE FIRST SUNDAY AFTER EASTER

The Collect
Almighty Father, which hast given thy only Son to die
for our sins, and to rise again for our justification: grant
us so to put away the leaven of malice and wickedness,
that we may always serve thee in pureness of living and
truth; through Jesus Christ our Lord. **Amen.**

The Epistle	*The Gospel*
1 John 5.4–12	John 20.19–23

THE SECOND SUNDAY AFTER EASTER

The Collect
Almighty God, which hast given thy holy Son to be unto
us, both a sacrifice for sin, and also an example of godly
life: give us the grace that we may always most thank-
fully receive that his inestimable benefit, and also daily
endeavour ourselves to follow the blessed steps of his
most holy life. **Amen.**

The Epistle	*The Gospel*
1 Peter 2.19–25	John 10.11–16

THE THIRD SUNDAY AFTER EASTER

The Collect
Almighty God, which showest to all men that be in error
the light of thy truth, to the intent that they may return
into the way of righteousness: grant unto all them that be
admitted into the fellowship of Christ's religion, that they
may eschew those things that be contrary to their profes-
sion, and follow all such things as be agreeable to the
same; through our Lord Jesus Christ. **Amen.**

The Epistle
1 Peter 2.11–17

The Gospel
John 16.16–22

THE FOURTH SUNDAY AFTER EASTER

The Collect
Almighty God, which dost make the minds of all faithful
men to be of one will; grant unto thy people, that they
may love the thing which thou commandest, and desire
that which thou dost promise; that among the sundry
and manifold changes of the world, our hearts may
surely there be fixed, where true joys are to be found;
through Christ our Lord. **Amen.**

The Epistle
James 1.17–21

The Gospel
John 16.5–15

THE FIFTH SUNDAY AFTER EASTER

The Collect
Lord from whom all good things do come: grant us, thy
humble servants, that by thy holy inspiration we may
think those things that be good, and by thy merciful
guiding may perform the same; through our Lord Jesus
Christ. **Amen.**

The Epistle
James 1.22–27

The Gospel
John 16.23–33

THE ASCENSION DAY

The Collect
Grant we beseech thee, almighty God, that like as we do
believe thy only-begotten Son our Lord to have ascended
into the heavens; so we may also in heart and mind
thither ascend, and with him continually dwell. **Amen.**

The Epistle
Acts 1.1–11

The Gospel
Mark 16.14–20

THE SUNDAY AFTER THE ASCENSION

The Collect
O God, the king of glory, which hast exalted thine only
Son Jesus Christ, with great triumph unto thy kingdom in
heaven: we beseech thee, leave us not comfortless; but
send to us thine Holy Ghost to comfort us, and exalt us
into the same place whither our saviour Christ is gone
before; who liveth and reigneth, with thee and the Holy
Ghost, now and ever. **Amen.**

The Epistle   *The Gospel*
1 Peter 4.7–11   John 15.26—16.4

WHIT-SUNDAY

The Collect
God, which as upon this day hast taught the hearts of
thy faithful people by the sending to them the light of
thy Holy Spirit: grant us by the same Spirit to have a
right judgement in all things, and evermore to rejoice in
his holy comfort, through the merits of Christ Jesus our
saviour; who liveth and reigneth with thee in the unity
of the same Spirit, one God, world without end. **Amen.**

The Epistle   *The Gospel*
Acts 2.1–11   John 14.15–21

TRINITY SUNDAY

The Collect
Almighty and everlasting God, which hast given unto us
thy servants grace by the confession of a true faith to
acknowledge the glory of the eternal Trinity, and in the
power of the divine majesty to worship the unity: we
beseech thee, that through the steadfastness of this faith,
we may evermore be defended from all adversity, which
livest and reigneth, one God, world without end. **Amen.**

The Epistle   The Gospel
Revelation 4.1–11   John 3.1–15

THE FIRST SUNDAY AFTER TRINITY

The Collect
God, the strength of all them that trust in thee, mercifully accept our prayers; and because the weakness of our
mortal nature can do no good thing without thee, grant
us the help of thy grace, that in keeping of thy commandments we may please thee both in will and deed;
through Jesus Christ our Lord. **Amen.**

The Epistle   The Gospel
1 John 4.7–21   Luke 16.19–31

THE SECOND SUNDAY AFTER TRINITY

The Collect
Lord, make us to have a perpetual fear and love of thy holy name, for thou never faileth to help and govern them whom thou dost bring up in thy steadfast love; grant this, for thy only Son, Jesus Christ's sake. **Amen.**

The Epistle
1 John 3.13–24

The Gospel
Luke 14.16–24

THE THIRD SUNDAY AFTER TRINITY

The Collect
Lord, we beseech thee mercifully to hear us, unto whom thou hast given an hearty desire to pray: grant that by thy mighty aid we may be defended; through Jesus Christ our Lord. **Amen.**

The Epistle
1 Peter 5.5–11

The Gospel
Luke 15.1–10

THE FOURTH SUNDAY AFTER TRINITY

The Collect
God the protector of all that trust in thee, without whom nothing is strong, nothing is holy: increase and multiply upon us thy mercy, that thou being our ruler and guide, we may so pass through things temporal that we finally lose not the things eternal; grant this heavenly Father, for Jesus Christ's sake our Lord. **Amen.**

The Epistle
Romans 8.18–20

The Gospel
Luke 6.36–42

THE FIFTH SUNDAY AFTER TRINITY

The Collect
Grant Lord, we beseech thee, that the course of this world may be so peaceably ordered by thy governance, that thy congregation may joyfully serve thee in all godly quietness; through Jesus Christ our Lord. **Amen.**

The Epistle
1 Peter 3.8–15

The Gospel
Luke 5.1–11

THE SIXTH SUNDAY AFTER TRINITY

The Collect
God, which hast prepared for them that love thee such good things as pass all man's understanding: pour into our hearts such love towards thee, that we loving thee in all things may obtain thy promises, which exceed all that we can desire; through Jesus Christ our Lord. **Amen.**

The Epistle
Romans 6.3–11

The Gospel
Matthew 5.20–26

THE SEVENTH SUNDAY AFTER TRINITY

The Collect
Lord of all power and might, which art the author and giver of all good things: graft in our hearts the love of thy name, increase in us true religion, nourish us with all goodness, and of thy great mercy keep us in the same; through Jesus Christ our Lord. **Amen.**

The Epistle
Romans 6.19–23

The Gospel
Mark 8.1–9

THE EIGHTH SUNDAY AFTER TRINITY

The Collect
God, whose providence is never deceived, we humbly
beseech thee that thou wilt put away from us all hurtful
things, and give those things which be profitable for us;
through Jesus Christ our Lord. **Amen.**

The Epistle   *The Gospel*
Romans 8.12–17   Matthew 7.15–21

THE NINTH SUNDAY AFTER TRINITY

The Collect
Grant to us Lord we beseech thee, the spirit to think
and do always such things as be rightful; that we,
which cannot be without thee, may by thee be able to
live according to thy will; through Jesus Christ our Lord.
Amen.

The Epistle   *The Gospel*
1 Corinthians 10.1–13   Luke 16.1–9

THE TENTH SUNDAY AFTER TRINITY

The Collect
Let thy merciful ears, O Lord, be open to the prayers
of thy humble servants; and that they may obtain their
petitions, make them to ask such things as shall please
thee; through Jesus Christ our Lord. **Amen.**

The Epistle
I Corinthians 12.1–11

The Gospel
Luke 19.41–46

THE ELEVENTH SUNDAY AFTER TRINITY

The Collect
God, which declarest thy almighty power most chiefly
in showing mercy and pity: give unto us abundantly thy
grace, that we, running to thy promises, may be made
partakers of thy heavenly treasure; through Jesus Christ
our Lord. **Amen.**

The Epistle
I Corinthians 15.1–11

The Gospel
Luke 18.9–14

THE TWELFTH SUNDAY AFTER TRINITY

The Collect
Almighty and everlasting God, which art always more
ready to hear than we to pray, and art wont to give more
than either we desire or deserve: pour down upon us the
abundance of thy mercy, forgiving us those things
whereof our conscience is afraid, and giving unto us that
which our prayer dare not presume to ask, through Jesus
Christ our Lord. **Amen.**

The Epistle
2 Corinthians 3.4–9

The Gospel
Mark 7.31–37

THE THIRTEENTH SUNDAY AFTER TRINITY

The Collect
Almighty and merciful God, of whose only gift it cometh
that thy faithful people do unto thee true and laudable
service: grant we beseech thee, that we may so run to
thy heavenly promises, that we fail not finally to attain
the same; through Jesus Christ our Lord. **Amen.**

The Epistle
Galatians 3.16–22

The Gospel
Luke 10.23–37

THE FOURTEENTH SUNDAY AFTER TRINITY

The Collect
Almighty and everlasting God, give unto us the increase
of faith, hope and charity; and that we may obtain that
which thou dost promise, make us to love that which
thou dost command, through Jesus Christ our Lord.
Amen.

The Epistle
Galatians 5.16–24

The Gospel
Luke 17.11–19

THE FIFTEENTH SUNDAY AFTER TRINITY

The Collect
Keep we beseech thee, O Lord, thy church with thy
perpetual mercy; and because the frailty of man without
thee cannot but fall, keep us ever by thy help, and lead
us to all things profitable to our salvation; through Jesus
Christ our Lord. **Amen.**

The Epistle
Galatians 6.11–18

The Gospel
Matthew 6.24–34

THE SIXTEENTH SUNDAY AFTER TRINITY

The Collect
Lord, we beseech thee, let thy continual pity cleanse and defend thy congregation; and, because it cannot continue in safety without thy succour, preserve it evermore by thy help and goodness; through Jesus Christ our Lord. **Amen.**

The Epistle	*The Gospel*
Ephesians 3.13–21	Luke 7.11–17

THE SEVENTEENTH SUNDAY AFTER TRINITY

The Collect
Lord, we pray thee that thy grace may always prevent and follow us, and make us continually to be given to all good works, through Jesus Christ our Lord. **Amen.**

The Epistle	*The Gospel*
Ephesians 4.1–6	Luke 14.1–11

THE EIGHTEENTH SUNDAY AFTER TRINITY

The Collect
Lord we beseech thee, grant thy people grace to avoid
the infections of the devil, and with pure heart and mind
to follow thee, the only God; through Jesus Christ our
Lord. **Amen.**

The Epistle
1 Corinthians 1.4–8

The Gospel
Matthew 22.34–46

THE NINETEENTH SUNDAY AFTER TRINITY

The Collect
O God, for as much as without thee, we are not able to
please thee: grant that the working of thy mercy may in
all things direct and rule our hearts; through Jesus Christ
our Lord. **Amen.**

The Epistle
Ephesians 4.17–32

The Gospel
Matthew 9.1–8

THE TWENTIETH SUNDAY AFTER TRINITY

The Collect
Almighty and merciful God, of thy bountiful goodness
keep us from all things that may hurt us; that we, being
ready both in body and soul, may with free hearts
accomplish those things that thou wouldst have done;
through Jesus Christ our Lord. **Amen.**

The Epistle
Ephesians 5.15–21

The Gospel
Matthew 22.1–14

THE TWENTY-FIRST SUNDAY AFTER TRINITY

The Collect
Grant we beseech thee, merciful Lord, to thy faithful
people pardon and peace, that they may be cleansed from
all their sins, and serve thee with a quiet mind; through
Jesus Christ our Lord. **Amen.**

The Epistle
Ephesians 6.10–20

The Gospel
John 4.46–54

THE TWENTY-SECOND SUNDAY AFTER TRINITY

The Collect
Lord, we beseech thee to keep thy household the church in continual godliness; that through thy protection it may be free from all adversities, and devoutly given to serve thee in good works, to the glory of thy name; through Jesus Christ our Lord. **Amen.**

The Epistle
Philippians 1.3–11

The Gospel
Matthew 18.21–35

THE TWENTY-THIRD SUNDAY AFTER TRINITY

The Collect
God, our refuge and strength, which art the author of all godliness, be ready to hear the devout prayers of thy church; and grant that those things which we ask faithfully we may obtain effectually; through Jesus Christ our Lord. **Amen.**

The Epistle
Philippians 3.17–21

The Gospel
Matthew 22.15–22

THE TWENTY-FOURTH SUNDAY AFTER TRINITY

The Collect
Lord we beseech thee, absolve thy people from their offences, that through thy bountiful goodness we may be delivered from the bonds of all those sins, which by our frailty we have committed; grant this, for thy only Son, Jesus Christ's sake. **Amen.**

| *The Epistle* | *The Gospel* |
| Colossians 1.3–12 | Matthew 9.18–26 |

THE SUNDAY NEXT BEFORE ADVENT

The Collect
Stir up we beseech thee, O Lord, the wills of thy faithful people, that they, plenteously bringing forth the fruit of good works, may of thee be plenteously rewarded; through Jesus Christ our Lord. **Amen.**

| *The Epistle* | *The Gospel* |
| Romans 11.13–24 | John 6.5–14 |

ST ANDREW'S DAY
30 NOVEMBER

The Collect
Almighty God, which hast given such grace to thy apostle
Saint Andrew, that he counted the sharp and painful death
of the cross to be an high honour, and a great glory:
grant us to take and esteem all troubles and adversities
which shall come unto us for thy sake, as things profitable
for us toward the obtaining of everlasting life; through
Jesus Christ our Lord. **Amen.**

The Epistle   *The Gospel*
Romans 10.9–21   Matthew 4.18–22

ST THOMAS THE APOSTLE
21 DECEMBER

The Collect
Almighty everliving God, which for the more confirmation of the faith didst suffer thy holy apostle Thomas to
be doubtful in thy Son's resurrection: grant us so perfectly, and without all doubt, to believe in thy Son Jesus
Christ, that our faith in thy sight never be reproved; hear
us, O Lord, through the same Jesus Christ, to whom with
thee and the Holy Ghost be all honour and glory, now
and for evermore. **Amen.**

The Epistle   *The Gospel*
Ephesians 2.19–22   John 20.24–31

THE CONVERSION OF ST PAUL
25 JANUARY

The Collect
God, which hast taught all the world, through the
preaching of thy blessed apostle Saint Paul: grant, we
beseech thee, that we which have his wonderful con-
version in remembrance, may follow and fulfill the holy
doctrine that he taught; through Jesus Christ our Lord.
Amen.

The Epistle
Acts 9.1–22

The Gospel
Matthew 19.27–30

THE PURIFICATION OF ST MARY THE VIRGIN
2 FEBRUARY

The Collect
Almighty and everlasting God, we humbly beseech thy
majesty, that as thy only-begotten Son was this day
presented in the temple in the substance of our flesh: so
grant that we may be presented unto thee with pure and
clear minds; by Jesus Christ our Lord. **Amen.**

The Epistle
1 Peter 2.1–10

The Gospel
Luke 2.22–33

ST MATTHIAS' DAY
24 FEBRUARY

The Collect
Almighty God, which in the place of the traitor Judas, didst choose thy faithful servant Matthias to be of the number of thy twelve apostles: grant that thy church, being always preserved from false apostles, may be ordered and guided by faithful and true pastors; through Jesus Christ our Lord. **Amen.**

The Epistle
Acts 1.15–26

The Gospel
Matthew 11.25–30

THE ANNUNCIATION OF THE VIRGIN MARY
25 MARCH

The Collect
We beseech thee, Lord, pour thy grace into our hearts; that, as we have known Christ, thy son's incarnation, by the message of an angel, so by his cross and passion we may be brought unto the glory of his resurrection; through the same Christ our Lord. **Amen.**

The Epistle
Galatians 4.1–5

The Gospel
Luke 1.26–38

ST MARK'S DAY
25 APRIL

The Collect
Almighty God, which hast instructed thy holy church
with the heavenly doctrine of thy evangelist Saint Mark:
give us grace so to be established by thy holy gospel, that
we be not, like children, carried away with every blast of
vain doctrine; through Jesus Christ our Lord. **Amen.**

The Epistle   *The Gospel*
Ephesians 4.7–16   John 15.1–11

ST PHILIP AND ST JAMES
1 MAY

The Collect
Almighty God, whom truly to know is everlasting life:
grant us perfectly to know thy Son Jesus Christ to be the
way, the truth, and the life, as thou hast taught Saint
Philip and other the apostles; through Jesus Christ our
Lord. **Amen.**

The Epistle   *The Gospel*
James 1.1–12   John 14.1–14

ST BARNABAS THE APOSTLE
11 JUNE

The Collect
Lord Almighty, which hast endued thy holy apostle
Barnabas with singular gifts of thy Holy Ghost; let us not
be destitute of thy manifold gifts, nor yet of grace to use
them always to thy honour and glory; through Jesus
Christ our Lord. **Amen.**

The Epistle
Acts 11.22–30

The Gospel
John 15.12–16

ST JOHN THE BAPTIST
24 JUNE

The Collect
Almighty God, by whose providence thy servant John the
Baptist was wonderfully born, and sent to prepare the
way of thy Son our saviour by preaching of penance:
make us so to follow his doctrine and holy life, that we
may truly repent according to his preaching; and after his
example constantly speak the truth, boldly rebuke vice,
and patiently suffer for the truth's sake; through Jesus
Christ our Lord. **Amen.**

The Epistle
Acts 13.16–26

The Gospel
Luke 1.57–80

ST PETER'S DAY
29 JUNE

The Collect
Almighty God, which by thy Son Jesus Christ hast given to thy apostle Saint Peter many excellent gifts, and commandest him earnestly to feed thy flock: make, we beseech thee, all bishops and pastors diligently to preach thy holy word and the people obediently to follow the same, that they may receive the crown of everlasting glory; through Jesus Christ our Lord. **Amen.**

The Epistle
Acts 12.1–11

The Gospel
Matthew 16.13–19

ST MARY MAGDALENE
22 JULY

The Collect
Merciful Father, give us grace, that we never presume to sin through the example of any creature; but if it shall chance us at any time to offend thy divine majesty, that then we may truly repent, and lament the same, after the example of Mary Magdalene, and by lively faith obtain remission of all our sins; through the only merits of thy Son, our saviour Christ. **Amen.**

The Epistle
2 Corinthians 5.14–17

The Gospel
John 20.11–18

ST JAMES THE APOSTLE

25 JULY

The Collect

Grant, O merciful God, that as thine holy apostle James, leaving his father and all that he had, without delay, was obedient unto the calling of thy Son Jesus Christ, and followed him; so we, forsaking all worldly and carnal affections, may be evermore ready to follow thy commandments; through Jesus Christ our Lord. **Amen.**

The Epistle
Acts 11.27—12.3

The Gospel
Matthew 20.20–28

THE TRANSFIGURATION

6 AUGUST

The Collect

O God, who before the passion of thine only-begotten Son didst reveal his glory upon the holy mount: grant unto us thy servants, that in faith beholding the light of his countenance, we may be strengthened to bear the cross, and be changed into his likeness from glory to glory; through the same Jesus Christ our Lord. **Amen.**

The Epistle
1 John 3.1–3

The Gospel
Mark 9.2–7

ST BARTHOLOMEW
24 AUGUST

The Collect
O Almighty and everlasting God, which hast given grace
to thy apostle Bartholomew truly to believe and to preach
thy word: grant, we beseech thee, unto thy church, both
to love that he believed, and to preach that he taught;
through Christ our Lord. **Amen.**

The Epistle
Acts 5.12–16

The Gospel
Luke 22.24–30

ST MATTHEW
21 SEPTEMBER

The Collect
Almighty God, which by thy blessed Son didst call
Matthew from the receipt of custom to be an apostle and
evangelist: grant us grace to forsake all covetous desires,
and inordinate love of riches, and to follow thy said Son
Jesus Christ; who liveth and reigneth with thee in the
unity of the same Spirit, one God, world without end.
Amen.

The Epistle
2 Corinthians 4.1–6

The Gospel
Matthew 9.9–13

ST MICHAEL AND ALL ANGELS
29 SEPTEMBER

The Collect
Everlasting God, which hast ordained and constituted the services of all angels and men in a wonderful order: mercifully grant, that they which always do thee service in heaven, may by thy appointment succour and defend us in earth; through Jesus Christ our Lord. **Amen.**

The Epistle
Revelation 12.7–12

The Gospel
Matthew 18.1–10

ST LUKE THE EVANGELIST
18 OCTOBER

The Collect
Almighty God which called Luke the physician, whose praise is in the Gospel, to be a physician of the soul: may it please thee, by the wholesome medicines of his doctrine, to heal all the diseases of our souls; through thy Son Jesus Christ our Lord. **Amen.**

The Epistle
2 Timothy 4.5–15

The Gospel
Luke 10.1–7

ST SIMON AND ST JUDE
28 OCTOBER

The Collect
Almighty God, which hast builded the congregation upon the foundation of the apostles and prophets, Jesus Christ himself being the head corner-stone; grant us so to be joined together in unity of spirit by their doctrine, that we may be made an holy temple acceptable to thee; through Jesus Christ our Lord. **Amen.**

The Epistle
Jude 1.1–8

The Gospel
John 15.17–27

ALL SAINTS
1 NOVEMBER

The Collect
Almighty God, which hast knit together thy elect in one communion and fellowship, in the mystical body of thy Son, Christ our Lord: grant us grace so to follow thy holy saints in all virtues and godly living, that we may come to those unspeakable joys, which thou hast prepared for all them that unfeignedly love thee; through Jesus Christ. **Amen.**

The Epistle
Revelation 7.2–12

The Gospel
Matthew 5.1–12